THE MAKING OF A MUSICAL

Fiddler
on
the
Roof

THE MAKING OF A
MUSICAL

Fiddler
on
the
Roof

BY RICHARD ALTMAN
WITH MERVYN KAUFMAN

Crown Publishers, Inc., New York

For Dick, Garth and Larry

Library of Congress Catalog Card Number: 77–168311

Printed in the United States of America

Published simultaneously in Canada by
General Publishing Company Limited

Contents

94460

Preface

"THIS IS NOT JUST a show about Jews living in Russia in 1905, although it is that, on the surface. At its heart it's about the enduring strength of the human spirit—and man's ability to grow, to change, to overcome adversity."

I have given this little speech at the first rehearsal of *Fiddler on the Roof* in Tel Aviv, Amsterdam, London and Paris, and often my words were translated for a company of actors who knew little or no English. But since they did know that *Fiddler* had been a triumphant Broadway success, it seemed important that I attempt to tell them why.

In these foreign cities my job was to transplant Jerome Robbins's original conception by re-creating his staging. Each occasion deepened my awareness not only of how well Robbins had captured the essence of Sholom Aleichem's bittersweet stories, but also of how successful he had been in bringing the warmth and wondrous innocence of Aleichem's world to life onstage. Robbins considered the patriarchal and much put-upon Tevye, the role created by Zero Mostel, much more than an ethnic symbol. To Robbins he was also, and very importantly, a symbol of man's need to change with the times.

My association with Jerome Robbins and *Fiddler on the Roof* was the fortunate result of circumstance. Back in 1962 I directed Estelle Parsons in *Mrs. Dally Has a Lover* by William Hanley. The show received good notices, and during its run a great many uptown theatre people came down to Greenwich Village to see it, Robbins among them.

By coincidence he saw the show the same night Carol Burnett and her husband, Joe Hamilton, were in the audience. After the performance Carol and Jerry chatted, and with her Texas-style directness Carol asked Jerry what he thought of the production. He said it was extremely well directed.

"I'm glad you think so," she said. "Dick Altman is an old college buddy of mine." Carol and I were in the UCLA Theater Arts Department at the same time in the early 1950s and have been friends ever since.

Jerry's response was equally direct. He suggested that Carol have me get in touch with him. I did. We met and hit it off very well. Some months later he asked if I could assist him on his Broadway revival of Brecht's *Mother Courage*, starring Anne Bancroft and Barbara Harris. I was involved in another project at the time and couldn't accept his offer.

In the fall of 1963 I learned that Robbins was planning to direct a musical based on Sholom Aleichem's Tevye stories. I sent him a note, asking if he needed assistance on this one, and he responded that he did. I went to work for him almost immediately and remained with the show full time until it opened on Broadway.

Being a witness to and a participant in the creation of *Fiddler* was an onerous experience at times, but it was always enlightening. And it was a rare opportunity. As critic Clive Barnes of the *New York Times* wrote early in 1971: "Robbins is one of the seminal figures in the American musical theater. His work in the American musical will probably one day be seen as marginal to his total career. Yet, ironically, he is the most important innovator the American musical has ever known. . . . Works such as *West Side Story* and *Fiddler on the Roof* flowed from his sensibilities, and it became obvious that a major theatrical mind was concerned with the musical. It was as though Peter Brook or Jerzy Grotowski had picked up the form to fondle it."

No matter what great or how many talents are involved in a Robbins show, there is only one master artist. Everyone else becomes a color on his palette, which he uses when and how he sees fit. I doubt that all directors could or should work this way, but for Robbins there is no choice. It is the only way he functions at his best. And who can quibble if a show achieves the stature, universality and longevity of a *Fiddler on the Roof*?

To be part of a Robbins team, one must subordinate one's ego and to some extent one's talent. But chances are, one stands to gain more than lose. It probably doesn't hurt much ending up a brushstroke on a masterfully realized canvas.

R.A.

1

"We're a Cliché..."

THE STAGE of the Lyceum Theatre on New York's West 45th Street was bare except for an assortment of shabby rehearsal props that had been neatly placed by the production stage manager, Ruth Mitchell. The actual settings, with which the actors had not yet worked, were on their way to Detroit, first stop on the pre-Broadway tour of *Fiddler on the Roof.*

Actually, when the invited audience at this final New York run-through filed into the Lyceum that hot night in July 1964, the stage was completely bare. *Fiddler's* opening number, "Tradition," was to be performed in the show without props or scenery, the only technical aid being a turntable, which was also en route to Detroit by then. Ruth Mitchell and her stage managers, Jim Bronson and Bob Currie, accomplished the main scene shifts themselves, moving the various tables and chairs—all of which resembled wobbly Salvation Army rejects—as

1

quickly as possible so that the flow of the show would be relatively smooth.

Director-choreographer Jerome Robbins welcomed the audience and told them briefly what he felt they had to know: that the musical was adapted from Sholom Aleichem's stories about a Russian Jewish dairyman named Tevye, and that the action takes place in and around Tevye's farm in the village of Anatevka in 1905.

There was no orchestra that night, only a piano offstage to accompany the performers. The outlines of the three interior sets—Tevye's kitchen, the inn and the tailor shop—were marked on the floor with strips of colored tape (just as they had been during rehearsals) to orient the actors. Costumes were not used, only the rough, and by then ragged, rehearsal clothes the actors had been wearing to accustom themselves to the way their actual "period" costumes would feel.

The Lyceum is small, and that evening it was not completely filled. There were perhaps seven hundred persons in the theatre, filling much of the orchestra and spilling over into the balcony. The actors as well as the show's creators—composer Jerry Bock, lyricist Sheldon Harnick and librettist Joseph Stein—had each invited people who were close to them, personally and professionally, as had producer Harold Prince, Robbins and myself. The purpose of this run-through was to give everyone connected with the show a sense of how it might play to an audience.

Seeing a makeshift, half-formed musical can sometimes be exhilarating, because, lacking any physical trappings, it demands much from the audience's imagination. Since run-through audiences are predominantly show-wise, they tend to see more than meets the eye and are generally enthusiastic, often wildly so. A great many shows, particularly musicals, start out with more apparent potential than is ever realized in a full production. A few seasons back, A Time for Singing was cheered at its final New York run-through and Flora, the Red Menace was a triumph. But neither show left any mark on Broadway;

much work was done out of town but evidently not the "right" work in either case.

Knowing that run-through audiences tend to go overboard, it's often best to be wary of their partisan enthusiasm. But, for better or worse, we were not faced with that problem on *Fiddler*, for the reaction was noncommittal, polite at best. We couldn't help feeling disappointed and a little concerned by the overall coolness. If *Fiddler* was far from a smash that night, I don't think it was because the show lacked quality; more likely it was because of what people had come to expect of Jerome Robbins.

Here was the man who had masterminded *West Side Story*, a landmark Broadway musical. He had also directed *Gypsy* with Ethel Merman, *Bells Are Ringing* with Judy Holliday, *Peter Pan* with Mary Martin—and had been known as a Broadway wonder boy since *On the Town*, the musical he had created, along with Leonard Bernstein, Betty Comden and Adolph Green, twenty years earlier. His ballet choreography was world famous, and his sensational *Ballets: U.S.A.* had toured extensively after its 1958 debut at the World's Fair in Brussels.

Many people in that audience had been expecting a visually dazzling show from Robbins. Perhaps they had anticipated something of the explosive choreographic flash of *West Side Story* or the show-business pizzazz and brilliantly paced drive of *Gypsy*. Instead, they saw a stage full of drab-looking people performing something that seemed understated and tame. Without seeing the costumes and sets, it would have been difficult for *any* audience to grasp the unfamiliar and rather special atmosphere that *Fiddler* was trying to create.

And missing almost totally, at this point, was the show's symbol of ghetto life and its accompanying traditions: the fiddler on the roof. Jerry Robbins asked the audience to imagine that the fiddler was there, up on that roof, but Gino Conforti, who played the part, stood uncomfortably on a chair at stage center and Zero Mostel, who starred as Tevye, looked up to where the roof of the house and Gino would eventually be. The effect was hardly compelling. A fiddler on a roof might seem a precarious notion under ideal circumstances; on a chair he seemed utterly ridiculous. And Tevye's self-concocted dream with its ghosts and screaming villagers—a highlight of the first act—could not have been much fun, without the bizarre costumes and eerie lighting that had been planned.

Thus there was little magic that night and few clues as to what the show eventually would be. "There just aren't any high spots," a friend of mine said afterward. "It's okay, but I kept waiting for that socko scene, that showstopping number, and it never came. The show went along in a pleasantly mediocre way." This was pretty deflating, but it accurately reflected the general reaction that night. The show was so tightly integrated —every element affecting every other one—that it simply didn't work with so many of its visual components missing. And, at least at that point, there was no soaring musical moment that rose above the limits of the bare stage and galvanized the audience the way "The Rain in Spain" once had, or "I'm Gonna Wash That Man Right Outa My Hair." Jerry Bock and Sheldon Harnick have never been tunesmiths in the traditional Broadway mold. In writing *Fiddler* they were motivated entirely by their source material, taking great pains *not* to create songs that would violate the text or mood of the show.

Despite some disappointment, the New York run-through had no noticeable effect on the *Fiddler* company. The reaction had not been particularly reassuring, but neither had it been disastrous, and it was obvious that a lot of work would be done out of town. For the moment, the major concern was just getting to Detroit and putting all the elements of the production together in time for the opening, which was scheduled for Monday, July 27.

A couple of days after the run-through, the entire company, bags in hand, met at the Lyceum, boarded two chartered buses bound for Kennedy Airport and flew west. Most of the staff checked into Detroit's Park Shelton Hotel, along with leading actors Zero Mostel, Maria Karnilova and Beatrice Arthur. The rest of the cast was scattered among several small hotels near

"If you please, Reb Tevye. Pardon me, Reb Tevye . . ." Zero Mostel, *the man who created the role of Tevye, singing "If I Were a Rich Man."*

Courtesy of Jacobson & Harmon

The Fiddler *company leaving New York for the Detroit tryout, July 1964.*

the Fisher Theatre. Jerry Robbins, an inveterate moviegoer, went off to see a film soon after checking in, to escape, if only briefly, from *Fiddler*. But escape he did not. The film was *The Unsinkable Molly Brown*, and featured in its first big number, "Belly Up to the Bar, Boys," was Maria Karnilova, *Fiddler's* leading lady. At least Jerry could enjoy seeing her looking youthful and sexy, a far cry from the way she would soon appear as the wife of Anatevka's impoverished dairyman.

The next day, while the backdrops and traveler curtains were being hung, and the lights focused, the cast rehearsed with conductor Milton Greene and the orchestra in a building across the street from the theatre. Jerry spent most of the day with them, except when Ruth Mitchell or lighting designer Jean Rosenthal wanted to see him or have him approve something. Ruth had preceded us all to Detroit, and by this time she had the technical aspects of the show pretty well in hand.

Fiddler had been designed to fit the stage of the Imperial Theatre in New York, which meant that some temporary adjustments would have to be made to accommodate the theatres in Detroit and Washington. Although there were no major problems, Jerry tended to become edgy when anything affected the lighting. Jean handled him beautifully; she was always calm and placating, assuring him that whatever he wanted done would be taken care of.

She had worked with Jerry on *West Side Story* and *Ballets: U.S.A.*, and it was obvious that just as she knew him well, she also respected him greatly. Actress-dancer Sondra Lee, Jerry's Tiger Lily in *Peter Pan*, once said: "Jerry gets frustrated sometimes when he can't realize something on the stage or when he can't articulate what he senses in his mind. But even when he's tense, he can always be approached through humor. If you find yourself at odds with him, see if you can say something funny."

Jean Rosenthal's approach was somewhat different. Whenever he became agitated, she would look at him with a hint of a smile, as if to say, "You're overreacting," and he was always disarmed. There was a good give-and-take between them,

which suggested that Jean's equanimity was an ideal complement to Jerry's temperamental nature. She understood his needs
and, aware that the director's conception was paramount, did
everything possible to please him. Jean was a small woman,
dynamic yet at the same time quite gentle. When she died
some years later, Jerry dedicated a new ballet to her, *Dances
at a Gathering.*

The lighting for *Fiddler* was extremely important, more so
than for most other musicals, for it had to give shape and
dimension to a very special world Jerry was creating on the
stage. Boris Aronson's physical production was relatively simple
and uncluttered; there were few sets. What helped give it
richness and texture was the lighting—lighting to fit changing
moods, locales and times of day, and also to define each of the
four seasons. Long shadows were apparent at the onset of dusk,
and the fading sun cast a bronze glow. These effects, while not
drawing attention to themselves, added to the atmosphere and
helped draw audiences deeper into the action.

There were only two technical rehearsals and one dress rehearsal before *Fiddler* met its first paid audience—hardly
enough time to solve all the problems arising with sets, costumes, props, sound and orchestra. "Actually, we never technically rehearsed the whole show," says stage manager Bob
Currie. "We ran through the first act and did some work on
the second, but never got through it from beginning to end.
The first preview was the dress rehearsal of the second act. It
was a bit of a madhouse." Even so, despite *Fiddler*'s delicate
mechanics and the split-second timing required to revolve the
sets into place, there were few actual disasters in Detroit. One
night one wall of Tevye's house failed to close electrically as
the house began to revolve, and the wall was nearly torn from
the rest of the structure. Zero was making an entrance at that
moment; he rushed to the errant wall and sent it off in the
right direction, ad-libbing and having a marvelous time. Another night the show had to be halted for several minutes while
the turntable was adjusted so that the house set would not rip
a costly backdrop to shreds.

The opening-night performance went off without a hitch, however. It was livelier than the New York run-through had been; the jokes got laughs, and at serious moments there was rapt attention and some sniffling as well. During the second act lots of handkerchiefs emerged from pockets and purses— always a good sign. These responses, plus our own feelings about the show, were all we had to go on at first, for *Fiddler* had come to Detroit during a newspaper strike. The first published reaction to the show reached us a few days later in the weekly edition of *Variety*, and it all but destroyed the morale of the company. Under the "Show Out of Town" banner appeared a review that said rather bluntly that *Fiddler* was merely "ordinary."

The critic, who in true *Variety* fashion, was identified only by the first letters of his last name ("Tew" in this instance), considered the show "mildly amusing, moderately melodic and completely predictable." The music, he said, "seems ordinary and serviceable, rather than singable or haunting. None of the songs is memorable, many of them sound alike . . ."

Mr. "Tew" further cited the "ordinary" quality of the voices in the show, the "workmanlike" direction, the "pedestrian" dancing, the "lackluster" book and the "serviceable rather than spectacular" sets, costumes and lighting to support his thesis that the show was "no blockbuster" and that it "may have a chance for a moderate success on Broadway." It was a blanket condemnation, and being the only critical voice to be heard so far, it cast a feeling of doom over the entire company.

Everyone had hoped, of course, that *Fiddler* would not be just an ethnic show with limited appeal. Sholom Aleichem's stories had been read and loved by generations of Jews and non-Jews alike. If something so exalted and universal had become only "ordinary," then something was obviously wrong with what was being done.

Before and after performances, most of the *Fiddler* company gathered at the Normandy Restaurant across the street from the theatre. They began looking glassy-eyed and dejected. At dinner the night after the review came out, one of the actors cut through the silent gloom that enveloped his table to say, "Well, folks, we're a cliché—a show out of town and in trouble."

At the end of the first week Zero gave a party for the production staff in his hotel suite. People were not overly upset—there was no "out-of-town panic"—but a general state of depression existed. I talked with Sheldon Harnick, who had been sitting quietly in a corner, not looking very happy. "I'd kind of hoped there would be something special about this show," he said, "but I guess there isn't going to be."

The search for the problems began. There was no reason to doubt the effectiveness of Zero Mostel. Not even the *Variety* critic could contain his praise for Zero, calling him "extraordinary" and "superlative" at almost the same time. The first act was rich, varied and funny—and it had size; the major production numbers were all there. The songs worked, and the dialogue scenes were almost entirely effective. Act One had shape, and it was in good shape at that.

The trouble was clearly with the second act, which was long on pathos and short on humor. Worse, it seemed to let down badly, dragging the show steadily downhill toward its conclusion. It had more plot than the first act, but the drama was essentially small-scale and heavy—leaden enough, perhaps, to sink the entire show. The songs did not seem particularly strong or right. Everything pointed to a falling off of audience interest after the intermission.

The consensus was that the second act needed a *new* big number, something to pick up the pace and lift the audience's spirits. Actually the act already had *two* big numbers. One occurred at the end of a scene in the village marketplace that was basically pointless, little more than an excuse for the company to sing a peppy, jubilant song ("Anatevka") about their village. Eventually the scene and the song were cut (a shorter, slower and more poignant version of the song was later inserted and has remained in the act ever since).

The other big number, which everyone referred to as the "Chava Ballet," illustrated Tevye's torment on learning that his daughter Chava has run off and married a gentile. The sequence was ambitious and complex, involving almost every-one in the show. It lasted about ten minutes and seemed inter-minable. For all its originality and intricate choreography, it got little response from the audience, some nights no applause at all. The idea of dropping the number crossed a few minds, but since it was the only spot in the show where Jerry Robbins's choreography was expressed in ballet terms, nobody suggested cutting the number entirely. It needed trimming, of course, and much reworking, which was left to Jerry to accomplish.

For his part, Jerry seemed unfazed by the sour note *Variety* had sounded loud and clear. He continued to give detailed notes to the cast each morning after the previous night's per-formance, just as he continued his rigorous schedule of all-day rehearsals. It was clear, though, that he felt bad about the "Chava Ballet." He had toiled mightily on it, but as far as the audience was concerned, the show never seemed to recover from it.

Jerry began to make occasional snips in the ballet, but at the production meetings that followed each nightly perform-ance, Sheldon Harnick, Jerry Bock, Joe Stein and Hal Prince—each in turn—would say they felt the number was still too long. Jerry continued to feel hopeful about it, tirelessly changing and reshaping it. He also embellished it, adding subtleties and interplay between characters and finally great sweeps of actors whirling in and out of forest scenery, careening around the distraught Tevye—all of which beautifully reflected Tevye's state of torment. But none of the work could strengthen the ballet's emotional impact. What improved it most, sadly enough, were cuts. Little by little the "Chava Ballet" was shortened, stripped to essentials. The less of it there was, the more the audiences seemed to respond to it.

It would be fatal, of course, to let audiences dictate the terms of a show entirely, for they tend to differ from place to place. What works well in Detroit might fall flat in New York. Many musicals have received excellent audience response out of town —*Kean, I Had a Ball,* and *Henry, Sweet Henry* come to mind— only to arrive self-confidently in New York and be promptly

Zodiac Photographers

clobbered by the critics and cold-shouldered by ticket buyers. But audience response, if judiciously evaluated, *can* often be a fairly reliable measuring stick. For *Fiddler* the silence, the coughing or the perfunctory applause was helpful in telling us things about moments in the show that few members of the audience would have been able to articulate, if actually asked.

Audience reaction was also suggesting that some unexpected changes should be made. A big dance sequence in Act One, "To Life," took place in the inn during celebration of the news

"Anatevka," the jubilant version that was cut from the show in Detroit; left to right: Zero Mostel (Tevye), Maria Karnilova (Golde), Beatrice Arthur (Yente) and Sammy Bayes (Yitzuk the streetsweeper).

that Tevye's oldest daughter, Tzeitel, would be married. The number was exuberant and energetic, with much toasting and drinking, and at one point it presented an enormous pileup of dancers in the middle of the stage, with Tevye standing over them, a wine bottle in his hand, shouting "L'Chaim," a traditional toast and the Hebrew equivalent of "To Life."

Initially the pileup had been one of several climaxes, but when it literally stopped the show with applause each night, there was no doubt that the actual ending of the number would never top it. A new orchestration was written so that the number built musically, as well as theatrically, to this new final climax, and about a fifth of the number was excised. Jerry well knew how to quit when he was ahead.

The *Variety* critic had written that *Fiddler* was at least thirty minutes too long, and though it was painful to concede any points to him, nobody would have disagreed on the subject of length. Like most musicals, *Fiddler* had left New York overlong and was to be cut while in Detroit and Washington. Some trimming of the first act was done, but most of the cuts—about twenty minutes' worth—eventually came from Act Two, much of it from the "Chava Ballet."

Sheldon Harnick was particularly concerned that the show's length would work against *Fiddler*. He recalls that "when we got to Detroit, I was so nervous I felt certain that people were going to leave by the hundreds because the show was too long, as well as too serious and too Jewish. I was scared; Hal Prince was scared too. Just before we opened, Milton Greene had scheduled an orchestra rehearsal without checking first with Hal, and there was a scene in the lobby of the Fisher, with Hal screaming at Milton, 'Don't ever do that again! This show is too expensive, and I don't want any *more* expenses. If we don't get a good reaction here, I'm going to close this show so fast.' Oh, Hal was scared. On opening night we did lose a few people in the audience, but not many. Almost everyone stayed. Afterward I went across the street to the Normandy, and I stopped at a table right inside the door where the kids from the show were. Suddenly I said, 'Excuse me,' and went to the bathroom, and I locked myself in one of those booths. I sat down and first I thought I was going to faint. I sat there a few minutes, feeling dizzy from the tension, wondering if I was going to faint or throw up, and then I started to sweat. I sat for six or seven minutes with the sweat pouring off me, and finally I was okay and went back to join the party. This had never happened. I'd never had that kind of 'nerves' before."

On opening night I took fifteen or sixteen pages of Jerry's

notes to give the actors, writing as fast as I could on my lighted clipboard, with Jerry whispering in my ear and trying to watch the stage at the same time. By the end of the Detroit run, I was down to seven or eight pages a performance. With the cutting and tightening, plus the natural polish that comes from repeated performance, the actors and the show were getting gradually better. The changes Jerry was making were fine toothed, almost microscopic. He never mentioned the *Variety* pan, and people wondered if he had even seen it. They wondered, too, if the magnitude of the problem had even reached him. No one knew how Jerry really felt about the show, not even I, and I was at his side at every rehearsal and every performance. Was he pessimistic, optimistic, disturbed, downbeat, positive, enthusiastic? No one could be sure. He worked constantly, saying almost nothing beyond stressing the need to make day-to-day improvements.

We all knew it wouldn't be possible for Jerry or Joe Stein to come up with a radically altered second act. Since a great deal of plot had to unfold and be resolved in Act Two—the marriages of two of Tevye's daughters and the expulsion of the Jews from Anatevka—there was little that could be done to the book structurally. Thus it was less a question of constructing a new second act than of making what was there work. Generally, the details had to be sharpened and brightened, but no specific solutions seemed to be coming to mind.

Although Jerry wasn't saying much about it, he was working on a new routine for the male dancers. Late in the afternoon, after rehearsal, or at midnight, after a performance and the ritual production meeting, Jerry and his choreographic assistant, Tom Abbott, would go off to Jerry's hotel with Betty Walberg, the dance music arranger. Jerry would experiment with different dance steps, and once he was satisfied, Betty would write the music to fit them. This number was to be added to the wedding sequence—although what it was remained a mystery for a while—but since the wedding occurred in Act One, people remained unreassured. Why wasn't Jerry doing something grandiose and magical to save Act Two?

The actors knew they were not in an all-time disgrace or a one-night disaster. At best they felt a kind of cautious wait-and-see, without being hopeful that the show would ever achieve any stature. With luck it might be another *Destry Rides Again* or a *Redhead*, both of which limped along on the candle-power of their stars and soon were forgotten, not really flops but very minor achievements. Jerry Bock and Sheldon might have envisioned that *Fiddler* would fall into the same category as their *Tenderloin* of 1960, which had disappointed them the way *Greenwillow's* failure had disappointed Frank Loesser after the success of *Guys and Dolls* and *The Most Happy Fella*.

Zero Mostel, for his part, began behaving as though he had found himself in a turkey. The company's general cheerlessness gave him cause to grumble and moan, which he enjoyed doing enormously. It also gave him a wonderful excuse to be mock-furious with me, which I found funny and, strangely, almost looked forward to. Each evening, after the performance, I would come to his dressing room to give him notes from Jerry, and the moment I appeared he would holler: "Four eyes, get outta here!" or, "Schmuck-face, out!" or, "You're Robbins's friend—out! I want no friends of Robbins in here!" Each time, I would start to leave and he would call me back, offer me a glass of vodka and listen to what I had to say—not entirely in silence, however. He would continue to pour out invective, cursing me or Jerry under his breath. This was one of the games Zero played, and he played it to the hilt. Since he couldn't, or didn't dare, get at Jerry directly, he was satisfied to get in his digs at me. However, despite his snarling protests, he usually did what he was told. He was quick and precise, and he realized, however grudgingly, that in Jerry Robbins he was dealing with a talent that was at least the equal of his own.

There was no denying that Zero worked hard in the show. The role of Tevye is enormous, and Zero needed his rest, so once the show was in performance Zero attended a minimum of rehearsals. His understudy, Paul Lipson, who played Avram the bookseller, stood in for Zero at rehearsals. Shortly before each evening performance, either Tom Abbott or I would give

Zero whatever changes had been made during the day. Unlike many actors who are rattled by last-minute direction, Zero could digest and adjust to changes instantly.

As the Detroit run progressed, some improvement in the show's reception became noticeable. The coughing epidemic that erupted nightly, halfway through Act Two, began to diminish after "Do You Love Me?" went into the first scene and worked so beautifully. And as the "Chava Ballet" became shorter and shorter, there was less audience fidgeting and more attentiveness in the book scenes that followed it.

Slowly, at times almost undetectably, the show was getting better. A tiny but measurable increase in audience response could be noted with every change, and night by night the applause at the end of the show was better and stronger. Critically, the show was still in the dark—with only one notice, a bad one, to go on—and there was always the possibility of its being blasted by the aisle-sitters in Washington.

The actors were about the last to realize how much better the show had become. They were working very hard and were understandably weary. There were rehearsals every day, including matinee days, with no days off, not even Sundays when there were no performances. Resentment was building up against Jerry. If the show was going to fail, a scapegoat was needed, and Jerry the "slave driver" was the likeliest candidate.

Day after day he pushed the company, excoriating the dancers if they performed with less than maximum vitality, or Betty Walberg, when the dance music didn't suit him, or Don Walker, when orchestrations seemed too reminiscent of Tin Pan Alley. Sheldon Harnick recalls that at the first orchestra reading in Detroit "Jerry Bock and I were embarrassed because of the way Robbins took Don Walker over the coals—'This must be changed,' 'Rip that out,' 'Take this out'—and at the end of it we came up to Don kind of shamefacedly and said, 'Gee, we're sorry, we didn't know it was going to be like this.' And Don, who was beaming, said, 'Oh, this was an easy one.' He had been through it with Robbins before and he was very pleased, because on the whole Jerry liked most of what Don had done."

Jerry is not a diplomat. He says what he thinks without fear of hurting anyone's feelings. That's partly what makes him as good as he is. He doesn't waste valuable time or energy on niceties. The needs of a show always come first.

During rehearsals Gino Conforti was spending a lot of time in the audience, because the fiddler was being cut from scene after scene. Jerry was never wholly certain how to use this character. At first, the fiddler was to be a continual presence —invisible to everyone but Tevye—observing Tevye, reacting to Tevye's various conversations with his family or with God. But it soon became evident to Jerry that the fiddler was more of an intrusion than a presence. He was constantly in the way without contributing anything.

"What am I? Who am I?" Gino would moan. "I keep asking Jerry, but he won't tell me." Even if he knew then, Jerry was not ready to commit himself as to what the character would ultimately be. He was beginning to realize that he must use the fiddler sparingly, involving him only to underscore a suggestion of Jewish tradition. But I doubt that this instinctive shaping of the characterization was one Jerry could have articulated or explained successfully to Gino.

In the surprisingly successful East Berlin production of *Fiddler,* which opened early in 1971, the fiddler was a major character, a troubadour who reappeared before the audience to lead it from one scene to the next, and during the course of a performance he sang and fiddled no less than seven Jewish folk songs. This approach might have worked in East Berlin, but when I saw *Fiddler* in Copenhagen, I was appalled by a similar treatment of the character. The man who played the part was given star billing. He was a well-known Danish violinist, and at one point, much to the delight of the audience, he appeared before a closed curtain to play a mini-recital. The show ground to a complete halt and had a very difficult time recovering.

In Detroit the role of the village priest was continually whittled until it disappeared completely and the actor, Charles Durning, returned to New York to seek other work. This made

Gino more nervous than ever. Perhaps the fiddler's mission was to portray the age-old symbol of Jewish perseverance in the light of adversity, but Gino watched as his part became more and more abbreviated. And he wondered if, even though he had the title role, he would still be in the show by the time it opened on Broadway.

2

"What's the Show About?"

Fiddler's GENESIS dates back to 1960, according to the recollections of the three creators. "Jerry Bock, Sheldon and I had worked together on *The Body Beautiful*," says Joe Stein, "and I had worked with Jerry on *Mr. Wonderful*. The three of us were looking for a project to do together. That's how it began."

Sheldon remembers: "A friend of mine suggested *Wandering Star*, a novel by Sholom Aleichem about a Yiddish theatrical troupe. I read it; Jerry read it; we were intrigued by it and gave it to Joe to read. Joe said it was too big a book, impossible to compress for the stage. But since he was as interested in Sholom Aleichem as we, he suggested that we look at other material by the author."

"Then it occurred to me," says Joe, "that I had enjoyed reading the Tevye stories as a child, so I proposed that we consider them."

According to a diary kept by Jerry Bock, the trio met for the first time to discuss these stories in March 1961. "By July," says Jerry, "we had each read the Tevye stories and had met two or three times. Joe had sketched a rough outline, and we had begun negotiating for the stage rights to the material."

"Curiously enough," says Joe, "the basic story line, which I constructed at that time, is basically the one that's on the stage right now. It's never changed." Joe began work on the book itself in August, and on Rosh Hashanah (September 11, that year) Jerry and Sheldon started on the music. The first song they wrote was "The Tailor Motel Kamzoil," the background for Tevye's dream. During the course of the next several months they wrote nineteen more songs until they felt they had a "preliminary score" completed, but only a handful of these found their way, ultimately, into the show.

"What was unique about this experience, aside from anything else," says Joe, "was that it was the first time for any of us that a producer was not approached until after we had a rather completed piece of work. Up to then, and certainly since then, whenever I had an idea for a show, there would be a producer in the picture right at the beginning, but not on this show. If we had gone to a producer and said, 'Hey, we've got an idea for a musical about a bunch of old Jews and they have terrible trouble, and there's a pogrom,' he'd have thrown us out of his office, even though we were all fairly well known writers in the field. . . . When we had a fairly completed draft, we approached Hal Prince first, because we were closest to Hal."

"I read it," Hal Prince recalls, "and I had two immediate thoughts. One, ethnically, I have no background; I don't understand it so I can't direct it, and originally I was looking for a show to direct as well as produce, after all the years of being a straight producer, which I was beginning not to like. Two, I said, I don't think it's universal in its present shape. I suggested that they either get Jerry Robbins to direct it—because only he could give it the universality it needed, through the expression of movement—or else put it away and forget it. As far as I'm concerned, Jerry remains the only person who should have directed that show. Its structure is very worrisome to me; it always has been. And I still would say, 'Put it away if you can't get him.' There are not many projects you'd feel that way about, but I absolutely do about this one."

"By the way," adds Prince, "what we did instead, the very day we met, was agree to do *She Loves Me*. Jerry and Sheldon said, 'We've got this other show.' I understood that one because I'm an old Hungarian, so we went ahead with it." Work was suspended on the Tevye project for some months while Jerry and Sheldon did *She Loves Me*, with Hal directing as well as producing, and Joe wrote *Enter Laughing*. Although the Tevye project was dormant creatively, the search for a producer continued.

"Saint Subber was interested in producing it," Jerry Bock recalls. "So was Fred Coe, who was our next choice. Subber loved what we had written, but he couldn't raise the basic monies within a reasonable time, and of course Fred ultimately had that same problem. The history of this show, in terms of raising money, has been very difficult. Everybody thought it was far too special, too ethnic and parochial for any kind of open audience. The irony of the situation was that Fred was a gentile southerner, and he thought it was sensational. The least likely candidate, in terms of background, you would think would be Fred. But he was enamored of it and worked long to fund it but couldn't."

Ultimately, when Jerry Robbins actually did enter the picture, the situation with Coe became critical. Sheldon recalls that when Jerry would finally settle on someone he wanted— to design the sets, costumes or lighting, for example—"a month would go by, and we'd get a phone call from one of these people, saying, 'I thought you wanted me. Where's the contract?' This made Robbins very nervous. He said, 'I don't know what's happening with Fred Coe, but nothing's getting done. We're going to need a producer. Let's get Hal.' We said we'd already been to Hal and he doesn't want to do the show. But Jerry talked to him, and maybe it was because by this time we had more of a show, or maybe it was because of Robbins, but Hal finally said yes."

Coe agreed that Hal Prince should be his co-producer and was probably relieved to have him, but the relationship never quite jelled. Says Hal: "Fred was going to do the movie of *A Thousand Clowns,* and he was giving me very little time. I really felt it was silly: I was doing the work and I didn't want to have a co-production with somebody who wasn't available. Also, I had a feeling I'd be spending all my time on the phone being nice, and he wouldn't know how to deal with me either and would probably feel he'd have to be nice in return. He wanted to make a movie, and I wanted to do the show, so why should we waste time patronizing each other? I put it to him just as straight as that, and he agreed to let me buy him out, which I did. He has a substantial interest in the show, of course, and has made a great deal of money out of it."

With a full-time producer at the helm and a director committed to the project, work began in earnest in the fall of 1963, with a January 1964 target date tentatively set for the start of rehearsals. The show was to be capitalized at $375,000. In the 1970s, with inflation, it is not unusual for a Broadway musical to cost more than $750,000, so the tab run up by *Fiddler* in 1964 would seem a pittance to producers and show backers looking back on happier times. Actually, $375,000 was a bargain even then, for a show of *Fiddler's* size and scope could have been expected to cost a bit more. But Hal was a savvy producer; he knew when to spend money and when and how to cut corners. Even with new numbers added out of town and old ones dropped, there was very little waste, although a lot more than money was riding on the fortunes of *Fiddler.*

For Jerry Bock and Sheldon, for whom this was their fifth collaboration, the show offered the hope of regaining the stature they had lost in the two efforts that had followed their Pulitzer Prize-winning *Fiorello!* of 1959 (though the scores for both shows had been excellent). Bock and Harnick belong to that special breed of musical comedy writers who, when they go to work, do not set out to write a song so much as advance an idea.

"Once we choose a topic," says Jerry, "we do some initial talking, not knowing how long our talk will last. It lasts until

we say, 'Okay, we can start to write.' What I'll do then is work
musically on just guesses without any specifics in mind. It
might be a character in the play that I have some feeling for.
It might be a scene situation, or it might be general atmospheric
music that I write and see whether Sheldon responds or not."

"I wait for Jerry," says Sheldon. "He'll put anywhere from
a dozen to two dozen songs on tape. Sometimes he'll also talk
on the tape and suggest where a song might go or what character it might be for. And often I get a different feeling from
the music. Out of, let's say, twenty songs, I'm happy if there
are three or four I really like, and so is he."

"Initially," says Jerry, "the music is written first, and Shel
will set the things he responds to particularly strongly. But
eventually he'll start writing lyrics first, and I'll set those, so
that, overall, the pattern changes from music to which he writes
lyrics to lyrics for which I write music. Once we get to know
our show intimately, it seems that the lyrics—the *idea*—become
the propelling force. When we're at our vaguest stage, which
is at the beginning, I can pour out a lot of stuff and just give
Shel a grab bag of musical notions. But as we go on, he is called
on to cite case and point, the fact of a particular scene, the
character and so forth. Therefore I think that Sheldon, as the
lyricist, has the more difficult assignment, because he's always
dealing with specifics, whereas music itself is abstract. As the
composer, I can provide a musical framework in a less pressured
way, because I'm not rhyming or phrasing or coupling."

Sheldon admits that much of his life has been spent searching
for himself as a person and as a lyricist. The latter may have
been easier to achieve than the former, but the former must
certainly have affected the latter. One of his earliest and deepest
influences was E. Y. Harburg, whose lyrics for *Finian's Rainbow* had dazzled him when he first heard them. Since then,
he says, "I've wanted to say equally pertinent things in an
equally entertaining way." The day he finally met Harburg
he considers one of the most memorable days of his life—for
more than one reason. After hearing some of his work, Harburg
insisted that Sheldon should *not* write his own music, which
he had been doing until then.

Harburg's advice was devastating, for Sheldon had considered himself a musician since childhood when he studied violin. But he took Harburg's words to heart and after some soul-searching came to a similar conclusion. By then he had become an excellent parodist, and realized that he rarely wrote music unless he had a model to follow or parody. He also realized that he didn't think musically; the lyrics, specifically the ideas for lyrics, always came first. In writing of Jerry and Sheldon, author and critic Larry Swindell declares that "it was only after he began to supply verses to Bock that the full scope of Harnick's lyrical ability came into view. . . . He lacked the facility with music that was the birthright of his poetry."

Sheldon's double search—for himself and for his art—continued for many years after his first Broadway credit (the abrasively comic "Boston Beguine" for Alice Ghostley in *New Faces of 1952*) and well after he'd begun writing musicals for the New York stage. "As a writer and as a person, my life came together with *Fiddler*," he says. "I knew who I was and who Sholom Aleichem's people were, and where our lives touched." Jerry Bock remembers feeling "a sensation that you cannot question for you know it's inspiration," upon reading the Aleichem material. The project was undeniably right for both of them.

Bock learned some harsh but penetrating lessons in song-writing discipline from the three summers he spent at Camp Tamiment in the Pennsylvania Poconos in the early 1950s. There, along with other budding theatre talents—composers, lyricists, directors, designers and choreographers—he helped create weekly musicals, one for each of ten weekends per summer. "I ended up with a habit of writing quickly, under pressure, to assignment, within a short, crucial period of time," he says. "What I could not realize at the time was that I was exercising myself into good shape for future out-of-town try-outs of my musicals." Collaborating with Sheldon, Jerry wrote thirty-nine songs for *Fiorello!*, but only thirteen were in the show when it opened in New York.

The composers' next effort was to reunite them with the *Fiorello!* team: co-producers Robert E. Griffith and Harold

Prince, director George Abbott and his co-librettist Jerome Weidman. The project was an adaptation of the Samuel Hopkins Adams novel *Tenderloin*, a saga of New York's bawdy entertainment district in the late 1800s. The show was to be racy and razzle-dazzle, evoking a colorful bygone era. However, though the creators were the same, the formula that had successfully concocted *Fiorello!* fizzled. *Tenderloin* was a slick hodgepodge whose elements, many of them excellent, were totally at war with themselves. It was a decided disappointment and, coincidentally, my first opportunity to see Bock, Harnick and Prince at work.

In 1960 I received a Ford Foundation grant to observe the creation of *Tenderloin*. My specific assignment was to report on the way George Abbott built and shaped a Broadway show. Abbott was a legend by then, an unyielding and glacial wizard of Broadway know-how. He was incredibly fit for a man of seventy-three, and his towering height helped make him terribly imposing, but I was not fortunate enough to observe his work when he was at his peak. I quickly became disenchanted with his directorial methods, which to me seemed hopelessly mechanical. I was also surprised at his inability to come to grips with *Tenderloin's* problem-ridden book early enough to make it work. He blindly followed his own rule of changing little or nothing until a show went out of town.

Another of Abbott's liabilities on *Tenderloin* was his lack of rapport with its star, Maurice Evans. It was obvious, for example, that the two of them had never agreed on an approach to Reverend Brock, the character Evans played. Evans, in his musical comedy debut, proved to be a less than engaging song-and-dance man—a surprise, considering that he was said to have been the first choice, *before* Rex Harrison, to play Professor Higgins in *My Fair Lady*.

Tenderloin's book was the primary source of trouble, however, and because of it life out of town was far more hellish for Bock and Harnick than it would be on *Fiddler*. If the book was a failure, the only thing that could possibly rescue the show was the score. The pressure was never off the composers to keep coming up with new and better material. They worked around the clock, and as a result five or six of the best songs in the show were inserted during the Boston run.

"The main problem with *Tenderloin* was that it was done too fast," says Sheldon. "The experience on *Fiorello!* had been so good and there was such euphoria among Abbott, Griffith and Prince, Jerry and myself, that I think even before *Fiorello!* opened we were talking about the next show. They had the rights to *Tenderloin*, and we just plunged right in. For myself it was an eye-opener, because I really had not paid much attention to the books of shows I'd been involved with. On *Fiorello!* it was Abbott at his best; it was 'Daddy' taking care of all of us. So I figured he would do it again on *Tenderloin*. . . . Looking back on it, I can see that we didn't follow the original source closely enough. In the novel the minister is a small part, but we chose to make it the star role, which meant we couldn't shorten it out of town. And unfortunately, as it's been pointed out to us since then, the minister, though he was on the side of virtue and good, was a killjoy."

Cataloguing all of *Tenderloin*'s various production woes—the intrigues, tensions, casting errors, personality conflicts, muddled points of view—it is easy now, with hindsight, to see that the show was doomed to failure. But, as with any show struggling to get on its feet, those involved were much too close to it at the time to realize how bad things really were. The book was being doctored, but not everyone connected with the show was certain exactly how—or by whom.

There were two brothers who were also "observers" of the production. At first, I couldn't understand why they were so pointedly chilly to me, but I later learned that, quietly and quite unofficially, they were working on the book, and no one was supposed to know about it. James and William Goldman survived the experience and, among other things, went on to write respectively *The Lion in Winter* and *Butch Cassidy and the Sundance Kid*.

To earn my grant, the Ford Foundation directors asked that I keep a detailed record of my observations. The following excerpts from my journal suggest, if nothing else, that *Fiddler* had smooth sailing compared to its predecessor. And my first entry, dated August 10, 1960, was ominous indeed: "I don't know why they're going into rehearsal with this wooden script."

Here are some other entries, starting with *Tenderloin*'s rehearsals and ending with its opening night in New York:

8/17—Abbott blocked huge crowd scene, juggling groups of twenty-five people extemporaneously. After twenty minutes everything was working, with much detail. Incredible!

8/22—I begin to think Abbott is definitely handling Ron [Husmann] incorrectly. He gives Ron line readings, but Ron parrots and doesn't know what he's saying or thinking or feeling.

9/2 —Am increasingly annoyed by Abbott's handling of Ron. In beach scene with Evans, Abbott told Ron to hang his head, pause, smile and turn—but never discussed what he should be feeling.

9/6 —Run-through with audience. Score went over generally well, but audience not really with the show. . . . Book doesn't work; it's hokey, melodramatic. Everyone too pleased that Stephen Sondheim was positive and enthusiastic afterward. Are they getting a false sense of security?

9/7 —Arrived New Haven. . . . Evans seems tense and resigned. . . . [Set designer Cecil] Beaton is aloof and distant toward everyone.

9/10—The orgy scene just laid there, as did Act I finale. Restlessness during Act II, little applause at end. . . . I don't see how they can ever make this book work.

9/12—Opening night . . . reaction very mild. Meeting held afterward: Prince seemed disturbed, no one else appeared to be. All were pussyfooting and discussing details until Abbott said, "Gentlemen, I had a concept for this show and it doesn't work. Any suggestions?"

9/13—It is increasingly obvious that the Goldmans are heavily involved.

9/14—*Variety* review appeared today: a pan.

9/16—Very little concrete improvement has been made in New Haven . . . will be the same basic show for Boston, with the same basic problems.

9/18—Boston. Evans apparently objecting to new prologue . . . much secret scurrying around, meetings and re-writing of prologue going on. . . . Bobby Griffith to Prince, "Well, then, YOU get him to do it!"

9/20—Opening night. Big improvement, thanks to new opening number. . . . If the rest of Act I could be strengthened with new numbers, there could be hope, though the book is still nowhere.

9/21—Boston reviews: three favorable, three pans . . . *Christian Science Monitor* accurately picking up the hollowness and the problem of trying to be on the side of virtue with vice being more entertaining. So much depends on new songs, IF show can be saved at all.

9/25—There seems to be a movement to place entire blame on Evans. . . . Neither Abbott nor Evans has ever been clear as to WHO Brock is or WHAT he is.

9/26—Evans depressed and couldn't (or wouldn't) learn lyrics. . . . Finally Abbott told him to carry the lyrics and pretend they're letters from parishioners. . . . Prince says Abbott afraid to make changes now because Evans such a slow study.

9/28—Act I finale much better with "How the Money Changes Hands" . . .

9/30—Everyone optimistic today. New song, "Dear Friend," sounds excellent. People feel they've got a hit. Hal says "the word" on the show from New York is good now. . . . Evans still flubbing his words but seems happier with his role and the show.

10/1 —New York reviews of *Irma La Douce*, being good, depressed everyone . . . that show apparently deals with prostitutes and vice in a clever, original way, which can point up emptiness of *Tenderloin*.

10/3 —"Dear Friend" into show. Charming. The number is a plus. . . . Trouble across the street with Jack Lem-

mon's *Face of a Hero.* Harold Clurman has taken
over direction, with Alexander Mackendrick just sitting by.

10/4 —Pepless performance tonight. . . . Clurman's first
move after taking over *Hero* supposedly was to try
and get rid of Lemmon.

10/5 —Evans displeased with opening speech; wrote his
own, which Abbott promptly discarded.

10/6 —Very difficult to sit through show by now, or to be
at all objective.

10/7 —New orgy won't go in. Abbott, Griffith and Prince
said no after looking at it. [Choreographer Joe] Lay-
ton now working on another approach to it that will
enter the show in New York.

10/11—First New York preview. Benefit audience—predictably quiet. Show definitely "off" tonight: technical errors, underrehearsed orchestra, pacing of numbers
and scenes slow, and Evans flubbing his song lyrics.

10/14—Deadly audience tonight. . . . Evans and Ron pan-
icked and barely got through confrontation scene.
They changed all the lines. . . . Second act was a
shambles. . . . New orgy doesn't work. . . . There
is an air of desperation around the theatre.

10/15—Matinee audience best ever . . . gave people hope
for Monday's opening.

10/17—Opening night. Audience applauded numbers, relatively quiet during scenes. . . . Four curtain calls.
After final call, Ron fainted.

10/18—The reviews: five negative (*Times, Tribune, Post,
Mirror, Journal*); two affirmative (*News, Telegram*).

Although Jerry and Sheldon never experienced the desperation on *Fiddler* that had so marked *Tenderloin,* they never
stopped trying to better the show. And the impetus for much
of their work, as they will concede, was Jerry Robbins. "The
thing that was the revelation about Robbins," says Sheldon,
"was how he worked. He was like the world's greatest district
attorney, asking us question after question, probing—'What's
the show about?'—and not being satisfied with the glib answers

we were giving. We kept saying, 'Well, it's about a dairy farmer and his daughters and trying to find husbands for them,' and he kept saying things like, 'Yeah, but that's "Previous Adventures of the Goldberg Family,"' and he didn't want to do that. I don't know who finally made the discovery that the show was really about the disintegration of a whole way of life, but I do remember that it was a surprise to all of us. And once we found that out—which was pretty exciting—Robbins said, 'Well, if it's a show about tradition and its dissolution, then the audience should be told what that tradition is.' He wondered how we could do it succinctly. Then he suggested that we create a song that would be a tapestry against which the whole show would play. So we wrote 'Tradition' because he insisted on it."

Says Jerry Bock: "I remember that number being the most difficult and taking the longest time to write. It came in bits and pieces. I don't think we were quite through with it some weeks before we were to go into rehearsal, and I don't think we thought it was going to be so good at the time, because it came so slowly and unsurely. It sort of unraveled like a ball of string."

"All I remember is that it was difficult," says Sheldon, "and also that I was nervous because I thought it's endless; it's too long. To me an opening number had to be snappy and get down to about three or four minutes, and of course I was terrified that the whole show was too long, and that it was going to be too serious and too Jewish and a disaster. But Robbins wasn't worried about that. As the number was getting longer and longer, I suddenly realized I was watching a man literally mold a number out of pieces. Joe Stein would give him some dialogue—I guess I had written the lyrics already—but I think Jerry Bock had to keep supplying him with music, and it took shape like a piece of sculpture."

If "Tradition" was the key to *Fiddler*'s meaning, it also served to unlock the door to further probing and greater depth. "Once we'd made the discovery of what the show was about," says Sheldon, "Robbins would say again and again, 'Well, if that's what the show is about, why isn't it in *this* scene? Why isn't it

in *that* scene? Why don't we see it in *this* character, or *that* character?' And Jerry's only weapon, if we all ganged up on him and disagreed at a certain point, was to say, 'Okay, do it your way. Get a different director'—which was maddening, and yet we had to trust him because he had a total vision. He drove everybody crazy because he had a vision that extended down to the littlest brushstroke in the scenery and the triangle part in the orchestra."

Later, at production meetings after tryout performances, Jerry Robbins would zero in on problems that required solu-

"*The papas.*" Left to right: *Maurice Edwards (Nachum), Charles Rule (Moishe), Dan Jasin (Schmeril), Zero Mostel (Tevye), Michael Granger (Lazar Wolf), Paul Lipson (Avram), Tony Gardell (Label) in the opening number, "Tradition."*

tions and pinpoint where the composers should apply their energies. If they were disappointed with *Fiddler*'s reception in Detroit, the disappointment never rattled them. "*Fiddler* for us was endless rewriting," says Jerry Bock. "There were no days off, no time to take much of a breath and see the show and wander away. There was always something to do."

The fact that they were always working earned them Robbins's considerable respect. I recall Jerry's annoyance with his friends Stephen Sondheim and Arthur Laurents, when he returned from Philadelphia after seeing a tryout performance

Zodiac Photographers

of *Anyone Can Whistle* with Lee Remick and Angela Lansbury. "They're not behaving professionally," he said. "They're much too satisfied with it. They're not *working*."

Jerry Bock recalls: "I felt a sense of quiet confidence in being able to write this score—probably the only time I've ever felt that way—because I was able to draw on my own background, my own memories of music I grew up with. I never felt the urge to research the score; I felt it was inside me. And I was delighted to have the opportunity for the first time to express

Tevye dancing with the Russian in "To Life," a moment of rare harmony;
left to right (foreground), *Lorenzo Bianco, Zero Mostel, Michael Granger.*

this kind of ethnic music I'd always had a friendship with. When I was a child, my grandmother sang folk songs to me, both Russian and Yiddish, and since then I've always found myself oriented toward Russian symphonic music. The Russian stuff in 'To Life'—that, too, was part of me. I've never analyzed it, but I find it hard to distinguish musically between Yiddish and Russian. I just called upon the juices and everything felt right, as opposed to *The Rothschilds,* for example, which was the result of a great effort at research, because I wanted to do a classical score. With *Fiddler* it wasn't a matter of specifics so much as a conglomerate spiritual feeling that this was an area I could express myself in. And, right up to the last, I felt that I would never run dry, because it was so much a part of me, and probably because I'd never written it before. I'm sure Sheldon and Joe had the same inner sense of the material's being right for the writer. It's not that any of us is Orthodox; it was the association, the comfort of having that instinctive knowledge about things."

Within a week of *Fiddler*'s opening in Detroit, Jerry and Sheldon brought in "Do You Love Me?" for Tevye and Golde to sing in Act Two. The song defined the relationship between two people who had been brought together through a prearranged marriage. Its theme harked back to the very tradition that had been sung and shouted about in the show's opening number, and against which Tevye's daughters were rebelling, one by one.

"I had this funny notion," says Sheldon. "I thought it would be great if he said, 'Do you love me?,' and she said, '*What?*' And when we were in trouble with the second act, I decided to try and turn this notion into a song. That lyric took me longer than any of the others, I think. I worked on it constantly for five or six days, just going for long walks and feeling very happy if I could do two lines in an afternoon. And I couldn't find a form for it. I gave it to Jerry almost as a dialogue scene, thinking that he'd ask for revisions to fit his own musical scheme. But Jerry found a form for it, and set it just the way I wrote it. Since it had started as a joke, I kept looking for a joke to end it with, but I couldn't find one. So I thought I'd end it on a note that was just honest and sweet, 'After twenty-five years/It's nice to know,' not knowing that *that* was going to be the joke."

Jerry and Sheldon performed the number for Jerry Robbins. He had some suggestions to make; some changes were needed, but in general he liked it. Zero liked it. So did Maria Karnilova. Everyone *liked* it, but no one was particularly excited about it.

The actors learned it, and Jerry Robbins staged it the afternoon before it went into the show. Staging the number took only fifteen minutes, and the only prop was a wooden bench. Tevye and Golde were to be seated on the bench as the number began; at one point Jerry had her stand up and then sit down again. It was very simple, but when Zero and Marusha ran through it we realized how very effective the number was. It worked even better than the composers had anticipated, and every audience loved it. It hooked them into the situation; it engaged them in the relationship between the two main characters. Until then there had been nothing in the second act to hook them.

"Each time I saw 'Do You Love Me?' performed in the show," Sheldon recalls, "I found that it brought tears to my eyes and I didn't know why. Eventually it occurred to me that I had written my fantasy about my own parents into the song —about the way I *wished* my parents had been. My parents were fighting all the time, and in fantasy I wished they had held hands once in a while and said, 'Yeah . . . I love you.'"

3

The Concept and
the Creation

FROM THE BEGINNING, Jerry and Sheldon had been faced with the need to be faithful to the tone and the context of their source material and still be lively and musical. Thus they willingly and lovingly subordinated their musical skills to the demands of the book. But fidelity to the source was not just the composers' problem; it was a need that very directly confronted Joe Stein. His job as librettist had been to take the separate Tevye stories and shape a single story line out of them —a series of events propelled by the successive marriages of three of Tevye's daughters.

Joe is a skilled craftsman, who by the early 1960s was a seasoned author of musicals. He had written *Plain and Fancy* and *Mr. Wonderful* before his three-way collaboration with Sheldon and Jerry on *The Body Beautiful*. Afterward he authored *Juno*, which was adapted from O'Casey's *Juno and the Paycock*, and a musical version of O'Neill's *Ah, Wilderness!*, which he called *Take Me Along* and which brought Jackie Gleason back to Broadway. The chance to work with Aleichem's material, the Tevye stories, was to Joe, as it was to Sheldon and Jerry, a kind of homecoming, a return to his roots.

"My parents had come from Poland to the Bronx, where I was born," he says. "The language of my home was Yiddish; my parents spoke English haltingly. I can read Yiddish; I've read Aleichem in the original language, but I'm much more comfortable with English. It was the English translation of Aleichem that I studied before going to work on the book.

"Actually, I was very careful not to have any Yiddish words or phrases in the script—and there are only one or two Yiddish words in any of the songs. But through the quality of the talk, the construction of sentences, there is a kind of ethnic rhythm without any Yiddishisms."

Joe's greatest burden in transferring Aleichem's prose to the musical stage was not the language but the need to lighten the action and still be faithful to the spirit of the source. Generally, the show follows a downhill path, as first the traditions and then the stability of Tevye's peasant village are eroded and undermined. In the first act Tzeitel, the eldest daughter, marries not her father's choice, the middle-aged butcher Lazar Wolf, but a poor young tailor, Motel Kamzoil. The act reaches a climax with the triumphant wedding festivities and then ends chillingly with a Russian pogrom. In the second act two more daughters compound their father's disappointment into grief—one by marrying a radical who is soon to be imprisoned, the other by marrying a Russian gentile. The show ends with a final blow to the stability of the villagers: The Jews are expelled from Anatevka.

"The original stories are really a series of isolated monologues that have no connection with each other, except that they revolve about the same central character," says Joe. "Relating story elements to the whole community, and what was happening there, was the key to merging the separate stories into one. The trick was to write as though the author was looking over your shoulder. You had to get the smell and feel of the author's work before you could begin doing anything with it. Once I started writing I really never looked at the original material again. That would have been like putting on a strait-jacket, which I wanted to avoid. You have to use your own muscles."

"I don't remember if I even had a title," he adds. "I never bother with titles until the last minute." But as the book was being fashioned and the cluster of events seemed to be centered on the kindly and imposed-on dairyman, a natural title evolved: *Tevye*.

That was the title I found on the first script for the show I read. But shortly before rehearsals began we were calling the show *Fiddler on the Roof*. Nowhere in the Aleichem canon is a musician said to be cavorting fancifully on anyone's house-top, but a painting by Marc Chagall—of an oval-eyed violinist seemingly dangling in space over the roofs of a peasant village —inspired the title change as well as the whole decor of the production.

"The title was absolutely suggested by the Chagall picture," says Hal Prince. "I think Chagall hovered over the look of the show for a long time. I remember being asked if I would try and get Chagall to do the ad, so I wrote him a letter but he never replied. Not long after the show had opened, Chagall came to the United States. I wrote him again, inviting him to see the show, and again he didn't reply. I suspect he thinks maybe we stole the show from his painting."

"I like to think that *Fiddler on the Roof* is my title," says Sheldon, "but I'm sure we all can take credit for it. One day we were with Hal, going through the list of titles, and he liked *Fiddler on the Roof*, and at that point nobody could remember whose it was originally. It had come up once and had been discarded. I tried at some point to write a song called 'Fiddler on the Roof' to explain what the title meant. It didn't work out as a song, so I wrote it as a monologue and showed it to Robbins, and he loved it. He gave it to Joe, who then reshaped it a little, and it became Tevye's opening monologue."

> A fiddler on the roof. Sounds crazy,
> no? But in our little village of
> Anatevka, you might say every one of
> us is a fiddler on the roof, trying to
> scratch out a pleasant, simple tune
> without breaking his neck. . . .

Joe recalls: "I was in Europe doing a TV series when I got a call from Jerry Bock, who said that he and Fred Coe wanted to show our project to Jerry Robbins. I had never worked with Jerry. I had heard various things that worried me—because his reputation is that he's marvelous, marvelously creative, but not the easiest man in the world to work with. I said, 'Well, I have nobody to suggest who could match him, so if he's interested, fine.' They approached him, and apparently he liked it enough to get started with it. And when I came back, I began working with him right away."

Sheldon remembers feeling similarly apprehensive: "We talked to Steve Sondheim, because I was a little nervous about working with Robbins. And Steve said, 'Jerry doesn't have the faith in himself to be articulate. But if you listen closely, and especially if you listen poetically, to the images Jerry uses—if you can get to him on that wavelength—then it'll be an astonishing experience.'"

Sheldon says: "It was actually the pre-production work that was so astonishing. And I finally realized that it was in those six months that the show was made—that period of endless probing and endless questioning, which I began to think must be caused partly by a deep feeling of insecurity on Jerry's part. He has a fantastic imagination for what will work on the stage, which so many people in the musical field do not have. And before he set foot on that stage he did as much work as possible, so that it would be right and he wouldn't be panicky in rehearsal or on the road. And it paid off for all of us. Those sessions with Robbins were remarkable. But they could also be painful, and the one who got the brunt of it was Joe, because when Robbins took the show he was least happy with the book. What the book had then was warmth and humor, but as far as Robbins was concerned, it was all too amiable. He wanted more conflict."

"Robbins would keep hammering away at particular book notions," says Jerry Bock. "Not specific lines as much as the concept of scenes, ideas, thrusts, where one would lead to another. And so a great burden of the assignment fell on Joe's shoulders. Once a new scene was created, Shel and I would then dig in and discover if it was musical or *where* it was musical. It was frustrating yet extraordinarily provocative. It was also surprising, because when we came to Jerry, we thought that we had a pretty good draft and that the changes would not likely be major ones. His reaction had been quite positive; then he began to throw questions at us, which we had to answer and very often couldn't. In trying to find answers we were stimulated to do new writing and rewriting, so that it got ever more exciting along the way."

Sheldon says: "The people who have only a grudging respect for Robbins would say that we didn't *have* to make those changes—that it was just Robbins wanting to have his finger in everything. I myself trusted him—that he was doing it for artistic reasons and not to satisfy his ego. He did do lots of reshaping—'Wouldn't it be better if you cut this, or if you put this here?'—but I always tended to agree with him."

Looking back on the meetings with Robbins, Joe remembers that the work was extremely detailed. "We went through the show song by song, scene by scene, character by character. Jerry is very painstaking, and sometimes I would take the same scene and write it three or four different ways—just fool around with it, really, to see which way had more spark. If he didn't like a scene, I'd ask that he let me take another crack at it and come up with a different way of doing it. Jerry would sometimes insist that we approach a scene some other way. He examined everything microscopically. Often we'd spend a long time on just one line, but that's his way of working. Very often I'd change things; then we'd go right back to the way things were originally—because it felt better to him once we had examined alternatives. That was the way Jerry worked. At times it was tedious having to go over material that you think is fine. But the overall effect was very rewarding, because the result of it was an improvement."

Two months before rehearsals began, Jerry gave me a copy of a letter he had sent to Joe. It was crisp, incisive and very specific:

BOOK CHANGES BY APRIL

1. FORTY PAGES OF SCRIPT MUST BE CUT. No arguments on this—this is fact. If this means cutting whole scenes, do it now before the physical production gets put into work, so we are not trapped later in an immovable situation. . . .

2. DRAMATIZE STORY OF TEVYE AS THAT OF A MAN IN THE STATE OF TRANSITION. This is the story we are telling; without it our show is just a touching narrative Jewish *Cavalcade*. There is a much more vital, immediate and universal one to tell, i.e., the changing of the times . . . and the conflicts and tensions made by these changes. Tevye's conflicts, his attempts to keep his traditions and still follow his heart are MISSING. . . . The audience must be strongly directed to Tevye's ambivalences and struggles, and you must dramatize the tension of his struggle to keep his traditions while being assailed by outside forces THAT ARE PROJECTED IN TERMS OF HIS DAUGHTERS AND THEIR SUITORS—which brings up the next point.

3. Tevye, Golde and Yente and all the side characters (rabbi, beggar, innkeeper, butcher, etc.) are all stronger, more colorful, theatrical and riveting than the THREE DAUGHTERS, their suitors and THEIR STORIES; therefore we lose WHAT the show is about—the changing times AS SEEN THROUGH THE THREE DAUGHTERS AND THEIR SUITORS. This should be the most vital part of our show, but in context becomes the most ordinary, conventional and colorless. What this comes down to is that the writing in the daughter-suitor scenes has to be as inventive, colorful and as high a caliber as the rest of the show. Work must be done to change the balance of this both in book and score.

4. THE THREE DAUGHTERS DISAPPEAR. Tzeitel is gone completely; who she is, what she is, what she wants and what she is like are hardly even indicated. Hodel's growth and change from a traditional girl with a mind to one who weds the revolutionary idea and is swept up by Perchik's vision is missing. Instead we have a sentimental love story. Chava is also colorless until her meeting with Fyedka. . . .

Jerry then went on to specify key revisions he felt were needed in individual scenes. He concluded his letter on this note: "All the scenes I haven't talked about are good but overlong, including the last one which will get to be monotonous with wagons and bundles continuously running along the stage, or *The Eternal Road Revisited*."

There was nothing in *Fiddler* that Jerry didn't feel could stand improvement. The show changed a great deal, during rehearsal and on the road, but I doubt that Jerry's consistent dissatisfaction with it ever changed very much. At best a Robbins response to a new line was, "Yes, it's okay, but it's not good enough."

Communication between Joe and Jerry became increasingly stiff as time passed; and during the dark days in Detroit they were speaking very rarely. It became Joe's custom to give new material to me, and I in turn would present it to Jerry. For Joe, this show was an obvious labor of love, dedicated to the memory of his father. With Jerry very aggressively and insistently in the driver's seat, Joe inevitably came to feel shut out of it. This is not an uncommon experience for a librettist, for even under the best of circumstances there are countless compromises that must be made when so many other parties—director, choreographer, composer and lyricist— are involved.

Much of the business of shaping a musical's book results from trial and error. Until rehearsals begin, and sometimes not until the show faces an audience, it's often difficult to know what works and what doesn't. Jerry's experiments in rehearsal were often highly complex, driving actors and everyone else into a frenzy. For example, early in Act One there is a scene in which Golde urges her husband to speak with Lazar Wolf. She knows, but he doesn't suspect, that the butcher wants to marry their daughter Tzeitel. Immediately after this exchange, Tzeitel urges Motel to speak with her father. She knows that a marriage is about to be arranged for her and warns Motel not to dawdle in asking for her hand.

In effect, these were identical scenes. In each the woman was pretending to be subservient to the man but was openly pressing the man to action. Jerry hit on the idea of playing the two scenes simultaneously, something that could be done easily on film by intercutting but would be difficult to bring off well on the stage. Golde and Tevye were at stage left, Tzeitel and Motel at stage right. First, there would be a line from Golde and one from Tzeitel, then a reply from Tevye and one from Motel, and so on. When this seemed clumsy, Jerry had the actors read pairs of lines, then four lines each. Hour after hour he worked, and he wasn't alone. Joe was with him, juggling words and phrases, adding material so that each of the speeches would balance the other.

It was obvious to everyone watching that Jerry's experiment was going to fail, but he went at it doggedly the better part of two days, with Joe trying frantically to keep up with him. It was extremely frustrating to watch, and all too easy for us to feel superior because *we* knew, at least, that Jerry was wasting his time. When the experiment finally collapsed and the actors returned to playing the two scenes as they had been written originally, we could silently congratulate ourselves and wish we dared toss I-told-you-sos at Jerry. Later I came to realize not only that Jerry must work this way but that, often as not, the result can be magnificent.

One day he felt like rehearsing on into the evening, which meant that Tom Abbott and I and the stage managers had to remain. So did the three daughters, for at 6:45—fifteen minutes before rehearsals normally ended—Jerry had decided to begin staging "Matchmaker, Matchmaker" at eight that evening. There was much scrambling to telephones to cancel dinner dates or theatre plans, and we all felt pretty grumpy. At nine o'clock I was still slumped in my orchestra seat, only half watching as Jerry played around onstage with a couple of mops and buckets and the three girls. He pushed the daughters this way and that, and as he seemed to have only a vague idea of what he wanted, it looked as though a fruitless evening was in progress and that everything would be changed the next day.

It was nearly ten when Jerry jumped down into the auditorium and called out, "Okay, let's run it." I forced myself to attention and watched the number. I was amazed. The number was performed that night just as it would be for years. All the pantomime and facile maneuvering with the mops was there, all the humor and charm—all in a couple of hours. Jerry never made major changes in the number, nor did he need to; it was exactly right.

Working with Jerry was often a supreme test of discipline. We learned to take the bad results with the good, accepting one as we applauded the other. It was not always easy to do this, and sometimes Jerry's driving nature got the better of us. His tireless trial-and-error tactics were particularly exasperating to Russian-born set designer Boris Aronson. Although only in his sixties then, Boris seemed to carry with him the double burden of incalculable age and ceaseless harassment—as though every setback, every criticism, was one more affront in a legion of insults. Boris had been designing shows for Broadway since *Three Men on a Horse* in 1935, having spent his first dozen years in the United States working in various aspects of New York's Yiddish theatre. Exceptionally talented and versatile— a painter and sculptor in his own right—he is as much at home designing operas as he is designing plays and musicals.

By nature Boris is an artistic rather than a technical designer. He is not concerned primarily with the way things work or how they are to get on and off the stage. In this respect he is fortunate in having as his assistant a very able craftswoman in terms of theatre mechanics, Lisa Jalowetz, who is also his wife.

His assignment on *Fiddler* was to capture the flavor and

special essence of Chagall and at the same time serve the spatial needs of Jerry Robbins. Conceptually, Boris and Jerry were quite close in their thinking. What conflicts arose between them were focused on Jerry's need for more and more space—a traditional source of stress between director and designer—and on the apparent indecisiveness that by then had become Jerry's hallmark.

For example, Jerry and Boris disagreed on the amount of space that should be allotted the interior of Tevye's house. Jerry insisted that what Boris had given him initially was inadequate, so Boris expanded it. At our next meeting Jerry's reaction, on seeing the new model of the set, was, "It's so big, it's taking up the whole stage!" In essence, Jerry wanted to have his cake and eat it too, but eventually Boris was able to give him the space he wanted *and* at the same time reduce the apparent size of the house—simply by reducing the size and sweep of the roof. Boris also redesigned the dining table, making its upstage end shorter and narrower. The effect was to heighten perspective and decrease the amount of space the table took, while still making it big enough to seem able to accommodate nine persons in the Sabbath scene.

If Boris found Jerry's prodding essentially irritating, Jerry was impatient with Boris's slowness to articulate feelings and intentions. Being quick as well as impulsive, Jerry had little tolerance for Boris's long explanations of what he was trying to achieve. When Jerry wanted changes, he expected them to be made without compromise; whereas Boris continually bemoaned the destruction of his "values." At times neither understood the other's specific demands or objections; a communication gap existed between them, perhaps a generation gap as well. But apparently no such gaps have separated Boris and Hal. Since *Fiddler*, Boris has designed four Hal Prince musicals: *Cabaret*, *Zorba*, *Company* and *Follies*.

According to Hal, "Boris has said it took him fifty years to discover that what he really wanted to do was build jungle gyms that had no life unless people were on them, and, of course, that's what *Follies* is. The idea started with *Cabaret*,

Graphic House, Inc., courtesy of Jacobson & Harmon

but very tentatively, for we still had the winches, the moving scenery and all that. Then came *Zorba,* and from *Zorba* came *Company.* It was an evolutionary process. We couldn't have done *Follies* without each of the earlier experiences. . . . I thank Jerry Robbins for Boris Aronson every day of my life."

It was always Jerry's feeling—with regard to sets, costumes, songs or scenes—that he should not settle for anything too quickly. He seemed to believe that if he agreed to anything readily, he might miss something—or he might not be taking advantage of every last chance to pick and choose. He and Boris would discuss the color scheme for a particular set, and Boris would agree to give Jerry exactly what he wanted. At

*Boris Aronson's evocative setting
for the interior of Tevye's house.*

the next meeting Boris would present something that was
very close to what Jerry had requested, but by then Jerry was
thinking differently. Maybe he wanted a sunnier feeling now;
perhaps he no longer favored, say, that particular shade of
blue. Perhaps he had new thoughts about the scene and new
ideas he wanted to convey. He would study the model set with
total absorption, constantly challenging himself, and a whole
new approach might come to mind.

It would never occur to Jerry that perhaps he should have
hatched his new ideas a week or so earlier, or that Boris and
Lisa would have to work day and night, into the wee hours,
to complete the revisions he had asked for in the short time he

had given them. He doesn't take into consideration the work
or the time that's involved; he doesn't necessarily consider
what is actually shown him. What he does see, of course, is
what it *could* be, or what it *might* be. He seems to say to himself, "We've got this now, and it's pretty good, *but* . . . what
if we tried it that way?"

This also applies to his handling of actors. He moves people
around, changes his mind, moves them a different way, changes
his mind again and then, if he wishes, goes back to what he
started with. As it happened, however, his Tevye in *Fiddler*
was an actor who is quick to learn and respond, and equally
quick to tire of repetition. Zero must have been more than a
little surprised to be used as a kind of chess pawn by Jerry,
whose direction—often at the first blocking of a scene—was
strict, precise, almost choreographed, only to be changed completely at the very next rehearsal. Zero contained himself as
much as possible, but obviously he was not accustomed to
being manipulated this way.

Other actors less secure than Zero found the ceaseless
changes and repetition completely enervating. They found
themselves behaving like automatons, pliable as puppets but
equally lifeless. Early in rehearsals I had lunch with Bert
Convy, who played Perchik, the radical student. He was feeling extremely discouraged. "I don't care how I play the scenes
anymore," he said. "If he wants it one way, I'll play it that
way. If he wants it another way, I'll play it *that* way. All I want
him to do is leave us alone."

Bert had other reasons to be unhappy, one of which involved a financial sacrifice he had made to be in the show;
the other involved getting a satisfactory song for him to sing.
He came out even, in effect, for he lost one battle and won
the other.

To play Perchik, Bert had bought himself out of a contract
to do *Damn Yankees* in St. Louis that summer, and it had
cost him a considerable sum. His agent lined up a TV commercial that would pay him handsomely, but to do it he would
have to miss one day in the early period of *Fiddler* rehearsals.

Bert explained the situation to Jerry, but Jerry wouldn't consider letting him go. In fact, Jerry wouldn't even discuss the subject. He wanted the entire company on hand at all times so he could rehearse whatever scene he wanted to devote attention to, whenever he felt like doing so. As luck would have it, the day Bert would have been doing his commercial, he sat idly by, not being called to perform, doing absolutely nothing except fuming at his director. From Jerry's standpoint, however, to have let Bert go would have set a precedent, for others might well have wanted similar consideration, and ultimately the rehearsal schedule would have become jumbled and unworkable.

Bert and his vis-à-vis, Julia Migenes, who played Hodel, were the only two trained singers among the principals in *Fiddler*. Even so, creating songs for them to sing—numbers that defined them as characters and limned their relationship—was not easy to do. Jerry Bock and Sheldon engaged in some trial-and-error of their own in tackling this problem, which was only partly solved by the end of the Detroit engagement. Bert was still dissatisfied with the one number he had, "As Much As That," and he was not alone. "None of us were happy with it," says Sheldon. "It seemed a cartoony song, and it sounded like May Day propaganda—all about the people, the workers—so we knew we wanted to change it at some point."

On the plane from Detroit to Washington, Bert happened to sit next to me. He told me how displeased he was with his song. He also mentioned that there was a number in the show that he coveted—"Now I Have Everything"—which was being sung by Austin Pendleton when, as Motel the tailor, he wins Tevye's permission to marry Tzeitel. Austin was not a trained singer; the song was a strain for him, but it successfully expressed Motel's radiant joy at that moment. Austin got through it on energy and charm; Bert felt he could really do justice to it.

I was skeptical. There seemed no logical reason to take the song away from Austin, when it really worked so well for Motel. But Bert convinced me that the song was equally suitable for Perchik once Hodel has accepted his proposal of marriage. Further, he said, Austin needed a song that was better suited to his talents and even more appropriate for Motel, who, after all, was the religious Jew that Perchik was not. Motel's song should be more biblical, Bert suggested, perhaps making comparisons to David and Goliath to illustrate Motel's winning of Tzeitel from Tevye.

I had to admit that the notion was intriguing. I told him not to hold his breath but I would mention the idea to Jerry Robbins—as though I had thought of it myself—as soon as I got him alone in Washington. Later, before our first rehearsal began, Jerry and I were chatting and I matter-of-factly presented the idea to him. He liked it and said he would mention it to Jerry Bock and Sheldon. Nothing more was said, but I gave Bert a cloak-and-dagger nod during rehearsal.

Three days later Bock and Harnick came in with a new song for Austin. It was called "Miracle of Miracles," and one of its verses went—

> When David slew Goliath, yes!
> That was a miracle.
> When God gave us manna in the wilderness,
> That was a miracle, too.

4

"Washington Isn't New York"

THE *Fiddler* THAT CAME to Washington, D.C., in late August of 1964 was not all that different from the one that had come to Detroit four weeks earlier. What was important was not how much had been done to the show but that the *right* things had been done. Material that hadn't worked had been thrown out, replaced by material that was working very well, especially the new music.

"Dear, Sweet Sewing Machine" had been the first song to be dropped. It was a sweet little song that expressed a very happy moment in the lives of Tzeitel and Motel: the joint arrival of their baby and a sewing machine for Motel's tailor shop. But the *Variety* critic had singled it out as a likely candidate for elimination, and though he was wholly unloved, he was not entirely unheeded.

"Actually, the audience cut that song," Sheldon explains. "When it was done in Detroit, there was like one 'applaud'—the reaction was literally that bad—and none of us understood why. Robbins's ultimate hypothesis was that it was too late for Tzeitel and Motel to have a song; their story was over by then. You can stop for a joke, but you have to get on to the next story. I remember, about a week into rehearsal, Robbins came to us and said, 'Something's wrong with "Sewing Machine"; I don't know what it is.' I loved the song so much my heart sank, and I thought, 'Well, it'll get better, it'll be all right.' But he kept saying something was wrong. He sensed that it wasn't going to work."

Also removed from the show were the marketplace scene and the jubilant version of "Anatevka," as were "When Messiah Comes" and "Get Thee Out"—both of which had brought the show's penultimate scene to a standstill. It was Sheldon's theory that "When Messiah Comes" made audiences uneasy, because it suggested that the Messiah should have a guilty conscience for taking so long to get here. Actually, the song had a lovely lyric and a clever idea behind it, but since its spot in the show followed news that the Jews were to be expelled from Anatevka, it halted the show's forward thrust toward the final curtain. One of the cuts, particularly upsetting to Bert Convy, was his song with Julia Migenes, "If I Were a Woman." And he was not the only one who missed it.

"That was the only song I was really sorry to see go," says Sheldon. "I fought for it, but Robbins was probably right. I think he felt that it took too long to say something that could be done in a gesture, in a little bit of dance. And his sense for that was unarguable."

Among the new songs added, along with "Do You Love Me?," was the slower, more meaningful version of the excised "Anatevka," which replaced "Get Thee Out." It was the last song in the show, expressing the villagers' vain attempt to deny the warmth and affection they felt for the place they had to leave. They try to disparage it, and they do admit that it hasn't exactly been the Garden of Eden, but

> Anatevka, Anatevka,
> Underfed, overworked Anatevka,
> Where else could Sabbath be so sweet?
>
> Anatevka, Anatevka,
> Intimate, obstinate Anatevka,
> Where I know everyone I meet . . .

The final insertion before Washington was a song called "I Just Heard," a one-joke number in which Yente and the villagers spread false gossip about Tevye's family. It was a throwaway number that might not have survived further pruning of the show, except that it always had an important function to fulfill: While it was being performed downstage, another scene was being set up behind the curtain. "I Just Heard" is essential to the production, but it has never rated inclusion in any recording of the *Fiddler* score.

Almost twenty years earlier, another Broadway-bound show had a similar technical problem, but the solution was somewhat happier. Costume designer Lucinda Ballard once told me that while *Annie Get Your Gun* was trying out in New Haven, it was discovered that some sort of transition was needed to provide time and cover for a scene shift. Irving Berlin was sent off to whip up something that could be played in front of a downstage curtain. The throwaway number he created in haste was "There's No Business Like Show Business."

Another song that is never heard on *Fiddler* albums is "Chavaleh," a brief but moving song that Tevye sings about the daughter he has just lost to the Russian boy, Fyedka. As he sings, his three oldest girls, their husbands, Golde and the fiddler appear in a sort of memory ballet behind an upstage scrim. The number was simply and delicately choreographed, and was all that remained of Robbins's once lengthy "Chava Ballet."

With this expansive sequence all but gone and the marketplace scene completely cut, the second act was primarily a succession of two- and three-character scenes. It was often joked that the biggest number in Act Two was the curtain call. But it was no joke that an imbalance existed between the two acts, and it was hoped that a big scene and accompanying musical number could be added to the middle of Act Two.

Joe Stein came up with an idea that everyone liked. A refugee tailor, expelled from another village, passes through Anatevka and agrees to sell his sewing machine to Motel. After the transaction is completed—Tevye peremptorily bargains on Motel's behalf—the departing refugee makes an over-the-shoulder remark about what he thinks of this sleepy jerkwater town: "Anatevka, hah! It's a mudhole!" The villagers react. Why should he malign their town like that? They've got all they need here, everything anyone would want. And as they start reciting an inventory of their humble possessions—a pot, a pan, a spoon, a fork—a musical number begins. It expands and swells until it involves most of the company, the full sweep of the orchestra and the percussive sound effects of various wood and metal kitchen utensils all being clanked together.

Jerry Robbins staged the sequence soon after we arrived in Washington, and in the days to follow, while he rehearsed the musical number (which never had a title), I worked with the two actors who were vying to play the refugee, a new part. One of them was Ross Gifford, a villager; the other was Gino Conforti, who was still in the show but whose role as the fiddler had become so tiny, that except for a brief appearance in the "Chavaleh" sequence, he did not appear in Act Two until the last thirty seconds of the show. Gino hoped to double as both the fiddler and the refugee.

When finally put together, the new sequence was to last about ten minutes. It gave the girl dancers a particularly lovely little segment of their own—their first opportunity to dance since the show's opening number. The refugee sequence was rehearsed almost daily during the two and a half weeks in Washington but was never performed there. Because of the time required for Don Walker to write the orchestrations and have them copied, the number wasn't scheduled to enter the show until the start of previews in New York.

About the only important development when *Fiddler* reached Washington was that by then the company was completely exhausted. A number of people had colds; some of the dancers were limping, having injured themselves in falls taken during the boisterous "To Life" number. Between appearances on-stage, a few of the actors plopped wearily on the floor in the wings, and the backstage area assumed the atmosphere of an army field hospital.

This was the first visit to Washington for many in the company. Although some had been hoping to remain in soft hotel beds for a day or two while the production was being installed at the National Theater, others—primarily those who could still walk without strain—had been looking forward to seeing the Capitol and touring the White House. But those who anticipated a sabbath of sorts hadn't counted on the relentlessness of their director. We had a few hours to get ourselves settled, during which time rehearsal space was lined up in a hotel ballroom on Fourteenth Street, around the corner from the old Willard Hotel, where most of us were staying. Soon we were fully at work.

A new Actors Equity ruling, which went into effect after *Fiddler* went into rehearsal, stipulated that all actors were to receive one day off each week, whether in rehearsal, out of town or on Broadway. Although the ruling barely missed affecting *Fiddler*, it never occurred to Jerry to give his people time off.

The show had closed in Detroit on Saturday, August 22. Workmen were taking down the sets, packing and loading them, within minutes of the final curtain. By the time we reached Washington the next day, the trappings were already at the theatre. The company moved into the National on Tuesday, a day that was spent adjusting the lights, accommodating the technical crotchets and acoustical demands of the theatre, and rehearsing with the orchestra. (Union rules prevented

Milton Greene from having more than a handful of musicians traveling with him; the remainder had to be hired locally—in Detroit and in Washington—to be replaced by still others in New York.)

Wednesday afternoon brought a matinee performance and *Fiddler*'s first Washington audience. It was made up mostly of middle-aged ladies who huddled quietly in a half-filled theatre. The show played smoothly, and the actors did well, but the ladies were so unresponsive that the house might as well have been empty. There was only a ripple of applause at the curtain call—the singularly worst reception the show had ever been given and all the more devastating because it had come from the first audience in a new city. Backstage, anxiety and pessimism reigned again; everyone feared that all the changes, deletions and additions that had been made in Detroit—not to mention the marathon rehearsals—had been for naught.

Fortunately, there was little opportunity to dwell on the "disaster." There was only time for a quick dinner break before the evening performance, which surprised everyone once again —but this time happily. The audience that night was extremely receptive. There were plenty of laughs and warm, appreciative applause. The show played no better than it had that afternoon; the only difference was that the theatre was completely filled instead of half empty.

Thursday night the critics came, and with Friday morning's reviews came an easing of anxiety—not jubilation, to be sure, but relief. "Joy, there is such joy in *Fiddler on the Roof*," said Leo Sullivan in the Washington *Post*. "Of course, to know joy, one must experience sorrow, so there is a lot of that, too. . . . As blended together by the inventive hand of director Jerome Robbins, the new musical which officially opened the season at the National last night is a beguiling folk tale set to music."

In the *Washington Daily News,* although conceding that the show "has lots of charm, plenty of laughs, sweet strains and melancholy strains," Tom Donnelly quibbled that "there ought to be a stronger, richer, more continuous flow of music.

One song that's a real rouser would be a help, or a ballad to set us humming and dreaming all the way home. Still, a show of considerable merit."

Harry MacArthur, in the *Evening Star*, said that "*Fiddler on the Roof* is, in fact, as much a dazzling show of its director's skills as of its star's. If this is a less-than-perfect musical, Mr. Robbins never lets it show. Before anything can go wrong, he turns the proceedings into a triumph of his alert mind over anything that might turn out to be the matter."

Passing an outdoor restaurant between the Willard Hotel and the theatre, I met Hal, Joe, Jerry Bock and Sheldon seated around a table, devouring the reviews. They were all happy, and it appeared that the dismal ordeal of the Wednesday matinee had been all but forgotten. However, there was a lesson to be learned from it, though I didn't realize this fully then. It is dangerous to judge the merits or the faults of a show (particularly a musical or a comedy) by the reactions of a partly filled theatre. People are more inhibited and less responsive when surrounded by empty seats. They have reservations about the show even before the curtain rises. They can't help fearing that if so many people chose *not* to come to the theatre, something must be wrong with the play. And their show-me attitude reaches across the footlights like icy fingers to touch and chill the actors.

Later I was to have a similarly traumatic experience with *Fiddler* in London. My Dutch Tevye, Lex Goudsmit, had made a very favorable impression on Richard Pilbrow, whose London production of *Fiddler* was to begin rehearsing soon after the Amsterdam version opened in December 1966. I was delighted with Lex's performance, and as his English was excellent, I urged Richard to keep him in mind, in case the English *Fiddler* was successful enough to last beyond the limits of Israeli actor Topol's contract.

Topol did leave the show after a year, and since Lex was still touring Holland in *Fiddler*, Richard had Alfie Bass take over. By the time Bass left *Fiddler*, Lex was finally free, and

Richard brought him to London. I flew over to work with him and a new Golde, Hy Hazell, before they went into the show.

Lex faced his first London audience at a matinee, and the theatre was only partly filled. The audience sat on its hands throughout the entire performance and scarcely uttered a peep. It was that Washington "disaster" revisited. At intermission Richard and I were pale. "Have I made a tragic mistake?" he moaned. "Could it be his English?" I wondered. "*I* can understand him, but it's possible *they* can't."

"What are you going to do?" Richard asked. "There's not much I *can* do," I said. "All I can tell him is that this was one of 'those audiences' and not to be concerned about it. However, I *will* urge him to watch his diction." Lex had been coached on his English for some time, and I had been frequently critical of his enunciation. Like anyone speaking or singing a language that isn't native to him, Lex tended to be sloppy at times, slurring some words and wrongly accenting some syllables. Topol had experienced similar problems when I worked with him two years before.

That night Lex's performance was greeted with shouts and cheers. He didn't miss a laugh and at the end was awarded a standing ovation. His performance was a triumph; however, his diction was exactly as it had been that afternoon. The only difference was that the theatre was filled to capacity. It was an experience that neither Richard nor I would soon forget.

Once past the successful Washington opening, all of us felt more secure. Certainly nothing worse than that Wednesday afternoon "disaster" could take place, but then something did. During the second week of the run, Zero came down with a virus that pulled him out of the show and plopped him right into bed. His laryngitis was so bad he could barely speak, let alone sing. On four hours' notice, after intensive coaching by one of the stage managers, his understudy, Paul Lipson, went on in his place.

As a rule understudies do not rehearse until after a show opens in New York. But since Paul had stood in for Zero at many a rehearsal, he was familiar with much of the blocking, and in Detroit, on his own initiative, he had spent lunch breaks working with the assistant conductor, so he would know all the lyrics and the orchestrations—just in case.

Everyone in the company was worried, and not only about the possible seriousness of Zero's illness. This was to be the first major test of the show's strength. Was *Fiddler* strong enough to hold together and work without its star? Or was it, as Zero himself so often implied, a one-man show—and without that one man (like Tommy Steele in *Half a Sixpence* or Joel Grey in *George M!*) there wouldn't be much of a show?

When the pre-curtain announcement of Zero's illness was made, there were the expected moans of disappointment and some refunds were requested. But most of the audience stayed to see the performance. Actors are usually good about helping each other through crises. When an understudy goes on, they will do all they can to lead him through a show. During the complicated "To Life," the male dancers pulled Paul in various directions, knowing that no understudy could possibly know every movement. And in the wedding dance, where it was important that Tevye be leading Golde, Maria Karnilova made it look as if Paul were leading her. He wasn't, of course, but he could count on her to make sure he was going the right way and turning at each of the right moments.

Marusha's most evident virtue in that number was in not moving like a trained dancer, which required a special kind of virtuosity. Jerry Robbins had always sought a measure of sloppiness in the wedding dance. In a complete turnabout, he harangued his people for appearing to have learned the dance too well. "Don't look like dancers," he exhorted them. And he nearly broke the spirit of his female dancers by excluding them from the number. He wanted the people dancing to be believable wedding guests, so he picked the older, heftier ladies from among the villagers—women who didn't move particularly well.

Paul survived his baptism as Tevye without stepping on anyone's toes or offending the audience. The laughs he got were

smaller than usual, but they were there, and there were sobs
from the audience at appropriate moments in the second act.
He came through with a modest, efficient performance, which
was all the more remarkable because of the short notice he had
received, and he continued to do well in the part during Zero's
four-day absence.

Throughout this period I made frequent visits to Zero's hotel
room to keep him abreast of changes that had been made either
in rehearsal or in the performances he was missing. He was
never nicer to me than he was during his illness. Though feeling weak and miserable, he thanked me graciously each time
for coming. He was simply too ill to dredge up insults or ex-
pletives. It took a lot of energy for him to behave outrageously,
and he was just too sick to bother. Everyone was so relieved
when he finally returned to the show that we virtually over-
looked an important point proved by his absence. *Fiddler on
the Roof* had worked without him; those four days had not
been a disaster! The show could indeed stand on its own two
feet, without Zero, and whatever success it might have in New
York would not depend completely on how long he chose to
stay with it.

In Washington Hal Prince assumed the role of outspoken
creative producer. He was well equipped to do so, having co-
produced *The Pajama Game* as a callow twenty-six-year-old
and having been at least partly responsible for a string of hit
musicals that followed it: *Damn Yankees, West Side Story, Fiorello!* and *A Funny Thing Happened on the Way to the Forum.*

When I first met Hal, on *Tenderloin,* my initial reaction was
that he *did* resemble Robert Morse. The actor had done an
outrageously funny caricature of a "boy producer" in *Say,
Darling,* a quasi-musical based on author Richard Bissell's experiences on *The Pajama Game,* Hal's first show. Morse's performance was so obviously—and accurately—modeled on Prince
that there was talk at the time of a possible lawsuit. And during
Tenderloin, as I watched the buoyant, effusive, always enthusiastic producer in action, I realized how well observed
Morse's impersonation had been.

But time has passed, and the growth and change Hal has shown during the past decade have been impressive. He no longer resembles Morse—his hair and beard are quite gray— and if he can be likened physically to anyone even remotely, it would be Jerry Robbins. With his exciting work on *Company* and *Follies* (each in conjunction with such formidable talents as Stephen Sondheim and Michael Bennett), Hal seems to have a clearer idea of where the Broadway musical should be headed in the 1970s than any other director or producer.

By the time *Fiddler* came along, Hal's partner, Bobby Griffith, had died and he was on his own—directing as well as producing his shows. But he never attempted to compete directorially with Robbins. In Washington, with *Fiddler* only a few weeks away from its Broadway debut, Hal's concern was not the staging of the show but its length. He felt strongly that judicious trimming was necessary to sustain audience interest and fend off somnolence, particularly during that book-heavy second act. He continually prodded the creative staff to go through the script as though with a microscope, and if any lines or even words appeared to be superfluous, cut them. "We don't want a shred of fat," he insisted, and he pushed the point relentlessly.

Ultimately, every excision, no matter how tiny, helped make the show tighter and fat free. It also sharpened audience response—so much so that when members of a non-Jewish club bought 90 percent of the tickets to one performance, they reacted almost as enthusiastically as other, more heterogeneous audiences had. The show was beginning to function like a precision instrument—consistently and predictably.

Because of this, spirits were measurably higher within the company. The tension abated, and an almost imperceptible laziness began to set in—as though actors felt confident enough to want to coast awhile. But Jerry was far too demanding to allow it; even a fractional letting-down in a single performance was intolerable to him. He feared complacency more than anything now.

"Washington isn't New York," he warned the actors repeat-

Zodiac Photographers

edly. "We've got a long way to go to make this a good show."
He worked them even harder now, driving them to keep up
the momentum he had created. And despite their weariness
and the many illnesses, they came through for him. Their earlier
hostility had gradually evaporated, though I doubt that Jerry
even knew it had existed.

A week into the Washington run the dance that Jerry had
been working on since Detroit was ready to enter the show.
It had been born at a Hasidic wedding Jerry and I had wit-
nessed, months earlier, at the baroque Ansonia Hotel on Man-

"Sunrise, Sunset." Tevye's eldest, Tzeitel, being married to Motel; left to right: Bert Convy (Perchik), Zero Mostel (Tevye), Leonard Frey (Mendel), Gluck Sandor (rabbi), Austin Pendleton (Motel) and Joanna Merlin (Tzeitel).

hattan's upper West Side. We had attended a number of these events, for they adhered strictly to the kind of tradition, in form and spirit, that Jerry hoped to re-create in *Fiddler's* wedding sequence. At each wedding we felt as though we had hurtled back through time and been plunked into another world. All the men wore black hats and long black coats, and long strands of hair (called *payess*) curled loosely about their ears. Their wives were gaudily dressed, often bewigged, and were always segregated from the men.

Every bride and groom we saw looked pale and sad-eyed—

A *break with tradition: Perchik (Bert Convy) dancing with Hodel (Julia Migenes) at the wedding.*

frightened, no doubt, because they were marrying total strangers. For residents of the Williamsburg *shtetl* of Brooklyn, who ventured into Manhattan only on special occasions, arranged marriages were still integral to Orthodox Jewish life.

At the climax of each nuptial ceremony, when the groom smashed a wineglass beneath his heel (an act that has a benignly sexual connotation), there was a ringing cry of *"Mazel tov!"* from the assembled guests. And then the frenzied merry-

making began, the dancing and clowning, while the bride and groom were carried about on wooden chairs. Jerry absorbed all these details and selected from them, without forsaking their validity.

One evening, during the entertainment that followed the wedding ceremony, a Jewish comedian did a funny dance while balancing an empty wine bottle on his head. Jerry said nothing about it at the time, but I remember the rapt smile on his face and his almost hypnotic absorption. The impression obviously remained strong with him, for to climax the exuberant wedding celebration in Act One, he added the relatively brief but intensely exciting "Bottle Dance," during which four male villagers did a spectacular dance with wine bottles balanced precariously on their heads.

"Everybody had a different scheme for keeping those bottles on the dancers' heads," says stage manager Bob Currie. "One idea was to use morticians' wax to stick the bottles firmly to the hats. Another was to use specially made hats to which the bottles could be tied. Other gimmicks were tried, but none of them worked, and Jerry finally said, 'Those bottles will damn well stay on their heads or they'll lose their jobs!' It was just the kind of challenge that all those boys needed." At some performances a bottle did drop, but Jerry anticipated this (although he fired no one because of it): By prearrangement the bottle-less dancer had to retire from the dance—to the good-natured jeers of the other wedding guests.

The night the number was introduced in the show, I stood at the back of the theatre with Boris Aronson and Jerry—between them, as usual. The bottle dancers performed with absolute precision and grace, and at the climax of the dance eight men in black silk caftans stomped and whirled with wild abandon. The applause that erupted at the end was tremendous, and suddenly I felt Boris tugging at my arm. I turned to him and saw that tears were streaming down his cheeks. "Any man who can do that," he said, nodding toward Jerry, "I forgive everything."

5

The Protracted Agony
of Casting

WATCHING A PROCESSION of actors perform scenes and songs
that one has heard dozens, perhaps hundreds, of times just has
to become a kind of torture. After months of attending auditions, listening to actors read all the major scenes repeatedly
(sometimes ten or twenty readings of the same scene in a single
afternoon), followed by eight weeks of rehearsal and four
weeks of performance in Detroit, the essential business of
viewing the show was becoming an interminable and much-
dreaded experience. By the third week in Detroit I was feeling
stir-crazy, trapped in the audience at each performance, but
it was reassuring to realize that Jerry had come to feel the same
way. He began to skip the matinees and mercifully suggested
that I do the same.

It was indeed a treat to escape from the production for a

few hours, now and then. I remember going to see a just-re-
leased film one afternoon, *The Night of the Iguana*. When I got
back to the theatre, I felt as though I was visiting people locked
in a prison. "Was Gardner any good . . . what did you think?"
they asked, starved, like lepers, for news from the outside
world—which they knew they wouldn't return to until *Fiddler*
had opened in New York.

After the excitement of the Washington opening had died
down and the novelty of being in a new city had worn off, the
nightly routine—sitting out front, watching the show through
glazed eyes—became even more of a punishment. At the fifth
Washington performance, just as Tevye was promising Tzeitel
to Lazar Wolf, Jerry leaned over, whispered, "I've had it" and
walked up the dark aisle. The first act wasn't even half over.
The next night, just as Motel was pleading for Tzeitel's hand,
Jerry said, "I can't take any more," and he was up and out.
He wasn't dissatisfied or angry, just bored. The repetition had
become excruciating. Much of the show was now "frozen," no
longer being tampered with; that these sections were being
performed consistently well made continued monitoring of
them even more deadening. In the nights to follow, Jerry dis-
pensed with salutatory exit lines; when he reached his satura-
tion point he strode out of the auditorium to fresh air and
freedom. I remained in my seat, feeling stuporous but continuing to take those notes I knew Jerry would want Ruth
Mitchell, Milton Greene or the actors to have.

The second act was even tougher to take, and during our
last days in Washington neither Jerry nor I returned to our
seats after intermission. To see any new material—new lines, a
changed exit, songs or dance steps that had been rehearsed
that day—we would duck into the rear of the theatre. While
watching, Jerry would whisper his notes to me; then we would
return to the lobby and pace aimlessly with Hal, Joe, Jerry
Bock and Sheldon, all of whom were as surfeited with *Fiddler*
as we. Almost nightly, at this point, Hal would buttonhole each
of the pacers and ask if he had found anything yet—lines,
words, pauses—that could be cut.

Despite the tedium, Jerry forced himself to sit through an entire performance two or three times a week. The creative phase was largely over, but his concern for the show was no less acute than before. His focus was now divided and subdivided among myriad details—the way a line was read, the proper emphasis placed on a particular word. And there were always technical details to attend to: corrections for the three men who manipulated the follow-spots (a particularly sensitive job, greatly affecting the smooth flow of a performance; an inept operator could destroy not only the mood of a scene but also an entire audience's concentration); new cues for Ruth to give the "grips" so scene shifts could be shortened; requests for minuscule costume changes—an accessory that needed to be brighter or better; lighting that was too dim or too harsh, too warm or too cool; music underscoring that came in too strong under a passage of dialogue; a segment of orchestration that still had too much Broadway pizzazz.

Often, too, he would become aware of something that, through weeks of rehearsal and performance, had never caught his eye or ear before: a faltering of the pace, a too-modern candlestick, a too boldly colored babushka that drew attention from a principal to a villager. Though weary of the show in general, Jerry remained tireless in pursuing the improvement of details. He was trying to elevate *Fiddler* to whatever image, whatever level of excellence, had existed in his mind from the very beginning.

He had started rehearsing *Fiddler* in June 1964, after spending most of the previous ten months auditioning actors. He had been exhaustive about seeing people, as though intent on auditioning every available actor in town. The creators themselves had been thinking of possible Tevyes long before Robbins began holding formal auditions. They remember considering a wide variety of candidates, including Howard Da Silva, Tom Bosley, Alan King, Julius La Rosa and Danny Thomas, who, according to Sheldon "was too wrapped up in television."

"I think Danny Kaye was our first choice," says Jerry Bock. And Sheldon recalls: "At one point, very early, when we were

Graphic House, Inc., courtesy of Jacobson & Harmon

A pause during auditions, (back row) *Sheldon Harnick;* (middle) *Harold Prince, Richard Altman;* (front) *Jerry Bock, Joseph Stein, Jerome Robbins.*

making out a list of people who might be right, Joe Stein said it was his understanding that Danny Kaye had always wanted to do this role. All of us thought Kaye was too mannered an actor, but on the basis of one film, *Me and the Colonel,* we felt perhaps he could do it. So Carl Reiner, who was a friend of Kaye's and who was in town at the time, called Kaye's home in California but never reached him. He talked with Kaye's wife, and when she learned that the show was about a man with marriage-age daughters, she said, 'Not interested. Danny doesn't want to play anybody that old.' Whether this was true or not we didn't know, but that's as far as we got."

How and when Zero Mostel entered the picture, no one seems certain, though Hal says, "I think *I* was the pressure for Zero." At any rate, once Zero's interest and availability became known, there was little doubt of his suitability, even if he didn't seem the precise physical realization of the discomfited dairy-man who talks to God. "We had an image at first of Tevye as a thin, gaunt man," says Bock, "but Zero in a strange way can be thin and gaunt . . . he has such great power."

If Zero and Tevye were not mirror images, it must be said that Zero set a standard for every Tevye who followed him. All of them tended to be fat rather than thin and gaunt, even though Zero's own girth could be deceptive. He weighed two hundred and thirty pounds then, but his bulk was reasonably well distributed over his six-foot frame; his corpulence, such as it was, did not weigh him down. He has delicate hands and tiny feet, and when he moves onstage he seems almost to float. There is a rubbery ease about his dancing that Jerry Robbins likened to the shifting of a tub full of Jello—a considerable feat for a man whose left leg had been badly mangled in a bus acci-dent a few years before. He never seemed to favor his leg when he performed, but offstage he walked with the aid of a cane, and he often left rehearsal early, or missed it entirely, when leg pains became particularly emphatic.

Shortly before plans for *Fiddler* began to jell, Zero had en-joyed two individual triumphs on Broadway. The first had been Ionesco's *Rhinoceros*, in which, without resorting to props or makeup gimmicry, he had transformed himself nightly from a man into a pawing, bellowing beast. It was a tour de force, and he won Broadway's coveted Tony award as the season's best actor. He won his second Tony in a musical for Hal Prince, Stephen Sondheim's *A Funny Thing Happened on the Way to the Forum*. That bawdy saga of Pseudolus, a Roman slave who uses guts and guile to buy his own freedom, was a far cry from *Fiddler*, but Zero was known by then to be a man of such ver-satility that it was felt he could do almost anything.

A *Funny Thing* had marked Jerry Robbins's first experience working with Zero. Hal had asked Jerry to come to Washington when that show, under George Abbott's direction, seemed to be in trouble. Although never billed in the program or in the ads, Robbins contributed much to the show's ultimate pace and style, notably the sensational opening number, "Comedy To-night."

"Zero and Jerry worked fine together on *A Funny Thing*," says Hal. "But their relationship was very businesslike. There was no affection passed between them at any point. Zero did his job and he certainly was conscious of what Jerry did to make that show work."

After observing him at close hand, Jerry knew that Zero's gargantuan personality could never be subdued completely in playing Tevye, but there were traits and qualities that both the dairyman and the actor shared. And as with the best stellar performances, the fusion of actor and role could very likely produce an interesting blend—a valid melding of two distinct personalities. Robbins knew he would have to make sure Tevye and Zero remained in proper balance, not letting the latter overwhelm the former. And this, he knew, would not be easy.

Although Tevye was eventually involved in eleven musical numbers, including two sung monologues, Zero was not cast because of his voice. He had been singing special material and patter songs since his early days as a nightclub performer, but he was not in the pure sense a singer. Even so, he possessed a good and intuitive musical sense and had more than acceptably performed his many numbers in *A Funny Thing*. He projected a kind of musical bark that was as remote from the polished *sprechstimme* of Rex Harrison in *My Fair Lady* as Harrison's voice had been from the robust baritone of Alfred Drake, who for years had personified the ideal musical-comedy hero.

If Mostel and Harrison had anything in common, it was the fact that they were primarily actors, and by the 1960s, mostly as a result of Harrison's great success, singing talent had become a lesser musical-comedy requisite. Acting skills and the force of personality were the major considerations then. More than a few top Broadway musical stars have conceded that they could never have begun at the bottom, in the chorus: They never sang well enough.

Zero Mostel was actually the second actor to be signed for *Fiddler*. The first was Austin Pendleton, and this was to be his second show in New York. His debut had also taken place under Jerry Robbins's aegis. He had played the mother-dominated hero of Arthur Kopit's *Oh Dad, Poor Dad, Mamma's Hung You in the Closet and I'm Feelin' So Sad* for four hundred hilarious performances. With his slight build, self-effacing stutter, pale face framed by horn-rim glasses and a pair of legs that seemed to move on folding ankles, he could have been born to play the poor tailor, Motel. Also, it was Sheldon's impression that Austin reminded Jerry Robbins of himself as a young man.

Motel is a particularly critical role in *Fiddler*, for the first act hinges entirely on the outcome of the Motel-Tzeitel-Lazar Wolf triangle. In addition, Motel experiences more growth and development than any other character in the show. He first appears as a timid, terrified boy, but in finding strength to stand up to Tevye—through Tzeitel and his love for her—he blossoms into a man and wins Tevye's complete respect.

The actor playing Motel had to be endearing and project the kind of likeableness that would make an audience root for him and empathize with him. Austin possessed all of Motel's special qualities, and his own vulnerability made him an early favorite with his fellow actors. Considering that he had worked as an actor almost steadily since graduating from Yale a few years prior, it was always amusing to see him shamble into a rehearsal wearing ragged pants, disintegrating shoes and a shirt whose collar was hopelessly frayed. The day the company first put on its humble peasant costumes, Austin was a shock to the eye: He actually looked more prosperous and presentable than he had before.

With Motel and Tevye cast, two significant hurdles had been overcome, but forty-four other parts remained to be filled— including singers and dancers, who would present casting hurdles of their own. And as the structure of the show was

shaped by the romances of Tevye's three marriageable daughters, these parts were of singular importance. The search for
young women to play them was thorough and seemingly endless. (Joe Stein's Tevye differed from Sholom Aleichem's in
having only five daughters instead of seven. The younger girls,
Shprintze and Bielke, were chosen during a single afternoon of
eliminations.)

The problem was in finding actresses who would be believable as teen-age Jewish peasants accustomed to the harsh dis-
ciplines of the ghetto and the hard work of life on a poor
dairy farm. They had to be totally free of obvious worldliness
and "actressy" sophistication. And each sister had characteristic
though often elusive qualities of her own that were to be
conveyed.

For example, there was the *shtetl*-reared traditionalism of
Tzeitel. Though only nineteen, she was the oldest child, and
she had to suggest a measure of maturity as well as some of the
flintiness of Golde, her mother, the woman she would one day
become. The girl cast as Hodel had to be a freer spirit, a spunky
creature with a sense of adventure; she also had to be an
exceptional soprano who could do justice to the beautiful and
demanding "Far From the Home I Love." Whoever played
Chava had to project an earnest and quiet sweetness, be a believable sixteen-year-old—and also be a trained dancer, for
Robbins planned initially to have the climax of Chava's ro-
mance with the Russian youth Fyedka, and its effect on Tevye,
expressed in the "Chava Ballet."

Additionally, the girls who were chosen would have to be
completely plausible as sisters, a requirement that disqualified
more than one able contender. So it was with some trepidation
that Jerry Robbins brought the first choices for all three roles
onstage together for the first time. It was noon on Friday,
November 22, 1963, exactly ten months before the show opened
on Broadway.

With Tom Abbott's help Jerry worked out some steps for
them, so he could see how they looked and moved together.
The authors and Hal arrived, and we all sat in the orchestra

as Tommy led the girls through the rehearsed routine. The result was quickly satisfying, and everyone felt cheered. The three girls—Joanna Merlin (Tzeitel), Anne Fielding (Hodel), and Tanya Everett (Chava)—were dismissed, and we broke for lunch. Seventeen other actors were scheduled to audition for a variety of roles starting at 3:00. The first was to be Beatrice Arthur, whom I was especially eager to see, for we had once worked together Off-Broadway.

Leaving the theatre I went to meet friends at the Lester Osterman office, not far from where auditions were taking place. As I entered the office I was struck by the sight of the receptionist sitting at her desk in tears, staring straight ahead. Everyone else was crowded around a television set listening to Walter Cronkite relate the grim and unbelievable details of the Kennedy assassination in Dallas. Along with the others, I remained by the TV set for the better part of two hours. When I realized I was due at the theatre, I rushed back, wondering if we were actually going to audition people, and thinking how trivial and stupid and unimportant it all was anyway.

A few actors, early arrivals, were huddled around a small radio near the stage door, listening silently to the continuing reports. I spied Bea Arthur standing near the stage, tears running down her face. She was pleased to see me, but it was far from a joyful reunion. As we embraced she said, "I can't audition. I just can't." Looking around at the other actors, it was obvious that, despite their restraint, none of them was in any better shape emotionally. If pressured, some of them probably could audition, I thought, but even if they did, I doubted that we, sitting out front, would be able to concentrate and judge them fairly or with any measure of discernment.

Ruth Mitchell and Tom Abbott arrived, remaining quietly on the sidelines. Then Jerry came through the stage door and looked around at all the faces. He went over to Ruth and asked her to cancel the auditions and dismiss the actors. A moment later Hal came down the aisle with news that all Broadway performances would be canceled that night. The show does not always go on.

When work on *Fiddler* resumed after that black weekend, everyone took some comfort from the fact that at least the final selection of the three daughters had been made. But this comfort was short-lived: Anne Fielding refused to sign a contract. She was newly married, and the prospect of touring for two months, away from her actor-husband, persuaded her to bow out of the show. Soon we were casting about for a Hodel again.

If two hundred young women were seen in the quest to cast three of Tevye's daughters, twice that number of young men must have auditioned for Perchik, the revolutionary student with whom Hodel falls in love. The character has so many conflicting qualities that for a time the role seemed impossible to cast. Perchik is a radical firebrand, as his view of life demonstrates; he is also inexperienced and insecure with women, as is indicated by his blunt and awkward marriage proposal to Hodel. Not many actors are equipped to portray bold and passionate confidence along with basic youthful innocence, and at the same time have a good, strong baritone.

The names of the young men who tried out for Perchik could probably comprise a Players Guide in miniature, and though the list is too lengthy to include, such names as Bob Dishy, Timmy Everett, Gene Wilder, William Daniels, David Cryer, Tommy Rall, Leonard Frey and Richard Davalos come to mind.

It wasn't simply the complexities of the role that defeated so many candidates; it was their appearance as well. Perchik is the only Jewish character in the show who comes close to resembling a romantic figure; however, none of the creators wanted anyone Hollywood-handsome in the part.

One of the strongest candidates for the role was Stuart Damon, among the more promising juveniles in town that year. Jerry was so interested in Damon's potential that he asked me to coach the actor privately before the second audition. (At Jerry's request, I also coached Larry Kert, the original lead in *West Side Story* and the eventual lead in *Company*.) In addition to being an excellent singer, Damon was an intelligent actor who actually had a Russian Jewish heritage. I quite frankly explained to him that the one obstacle to his being cast was his too-good looks. (He was very much a Cinderella's Prince Charming, a part he ultimately played on television.) I suggested that he come to the next audition looking as unpretty as possible, and the following week he walked onstage in a rumpled sweater, torn Levi's and old shoes. He wore a floppy cap, unflattering glasses, and was unshaven. Although he had to squint through the strange glasses, he read extremely well, and I felt confident of his chances. After he left the stage, there was a moment's silence, and then Sheldon spoke up: "Yeah, but take off his glasses and he's still Betty Grable." Damon was never mentioned again.

Little more than a month before rehearsals were to begin, there was still no Perchik (and no Hodel, either). It was the end of April before Bert Convy finally auditioned. He had done television and a few films, but except for a stint in *The Fantasticks*—a show that has kept many a young actor alive—he had appeared in New York only in flops, on Broadway and off.

After his first reading Jerry turned around to me and asked what I thought. "I think he's fine," I said, but what I thought at that moment was what an idiot I was. I had gone to college with Bert, but it had never occurred to me that he could play Perchik. Jerry asked him to come back a week later.

The day Bert returned was also the day of Julia Migenes's second audition as a possible replacement for Anne Fielding. Julia was a talented singer who had been performing since she was seven and now had her sights keenly set on the operatic stage. She wanted to work, of course, but having little serious interest in a Broadway career, she was totally relaxed—a rarity at auditions—and consequently her own delightfully unaffected personality emerged through Hodel's lines.

Following standard procedure, she read Hodel's major scenes with Ruth, who read tirelessly and well with all auditioning actors. Bert Convy's audition was scheduled to follow Julia's, and the moment he appeared Jerry jumped up and called to Ruth not to let Migenes leave the theatre. In an instant Ruth reappeared onstage with Julia in tow, her coat on and a rather puzzled expression on her face. Jerry asked her to read with Bert. They did both Hodel-Perchik scenes, and the chemistry was perfect. Although they gave a reading and not a performance, the two scenes came to life fully—for the first time. When the actors had left, Jerry turned to get Hal's and the authors' reactions, all of which were strongly positive. The months of searching had finally ended. Ten minutes later, Larry Kert came in and auditioned, but it was all over by then and Kert was never considered.

The role of Yente the matchmaker was subordinate even in the original version of Joe Stein's libretto, but it was an important role nonetheless, because the matchmaker represented the continuation of tradition in the *shtetl*. In defying custom and marrying for love, Tevye's daughters came to personify the effect of changing times. Yente represented the old order, they the new.

Yente was Joe's creation, owing nothing to Aleichem but flavor. The matchmaker in the Tevye stories had been a querulous creature named Ephraim, who had little to say that was funny. In translating Aleichem into musical comedy form, Joe felt obliged to make the matchmaker not only pivotal but entertaining, and so the sober Ephraim became the gabby Yente. Even the name had comic connotations—a Yiddish designation for a busybody (Joe's only concession to that "second language"). However, most of the potential Yentes who auditioned gave readings that were surprisingly flat and humorless. Only when Beatrice Arthur read Yente's monologues did the character's ceaseless babbling become genuinely funny, for Bea was a first-rate comedienne. Although there was just a hint that her presence might be a bit too American and a shade too contemporary, everyone was willing to overlook it—everyone, it seemed, but Jerry Robbins.

He had reservations about her. He never seemed as certain as the others that her quality would match that of the rest of his Anatevkans. He cast her—but with misgivings, and only because he could find no one else who had a grasp of the character. Throughout rehearsals and well into Detroit, however, whenever cutting was needed, portions of Yente's speeches were always among those being nibbled away by Jerry's blue pencil. As her part became shorter, Bea became increasingly frustrated. Her husband, director Gene Saks, was seriously ill with hepatitis, and the more her role was cut the less she felt she should be tied up in a musical trying out away from New York. But Bea remained with *Fiddler,* leaving it after a year on Broadway to do the role in which she triumphed, one ideally suited to her, the flamboyant actress Vera Charles in *Mame.*

Eventually I came to realize that Jerry had been right all along about Yente. In Tel Aviv and in Paris I was able to cast older, smaller women as Yente, and in both cases the character had more substance; her relationship with Golde and the other villagers had more depth; even the humor was richer and more apt. Alina Stranitska in Israel and Florence Blot in France each possessed the qualities that Jerry doubtless would have preferred—the matriarchal bossiness that was also true of Golde, combined with the philosophical and pragmatic insights that advanced age and maturity accord.

Like nearly every significant part in the show, Golde was extremely difficult to cast. It was a big role but not a star role, so no Ethel Merman or Mary Martin was having it offered to her. The woman who played Golde had to look old enough onstage to have a daughter nearly twenty, and be able to sing as well as dance. She had to be convincingly Jewish, earthy, and because she was married to a dreamer like Tevye, also be a tough, no-nonsense realist without seeming unpleasant. Golde was a tall order.

Nancy Walker, the veteran stage comedienne, had been among the first actresses to be considered for Golde. She had played opposite Zero in a TV dramatization, *The World of Sholom Aleichem,* so it made sense to take a look at her performance and also see how she had worked with Zero. A film of the TV show was obtained, and Jerry studied it carefully— then decided against Miss Walker. Years later she auditioned for Yente in the film version but lost the part to Molly Picon, who was perhaps the inevitable choice.

A colorful collection of New York's finest character actresses auditioned for Golde, among them Kay Medford, Kaye Ballard and even Bea Arthur. The woman who finally got the part was not known as a character actress. She had come originally to audition not for Golde but for Yente, and whether she had entertained serious notions about being cast in either role we never knew. Few of us took her candidacy very seriously.

Maria Karnilova was an old friend of Jerry Robbins. She had danced *with* him years earlier and *for* him later in his celebrated *Ballets: U.S.A.* She had also played the faded burlesque dancer who stripped "with finesse" in Robbins's production of *Gypsy*. She was no stranger to musical comedy, but she had never performed an important dramatic part on Broadway. She was auditioned mainly as a courtesy—and finally won the role by default. There was simply no one else who could do it. And no one, including Robbins, could then have predicted how extraordinary her performance would ultimately be.

Marusha was lithe and trim, with a strong, bony face that when made up properly could affect the haunted, hollow-eyed look of a peasant wife. Being a trained dancer, she was mistress of her body and very quickly sketched in the physical picture of a master sergeant in charge of a chaotic and unruly platoon. But the physical picture was only part of the characterization Jerry was seeking, and soon she was even having trouble getting that to work for her.

From the first rehearsals she seemed stiff and uncomfortable in the role. Being ill at ease heightened her stiffness and made it impossible for her to connect with Golde. Jerry worked with her patiently, but the more she rehearsed the more self-conscious she became, and, feeling inadequate, blamed the part for her difficulty.

During the third week of rehearsal I had lunch with her and Bea Arthur at a Chinese restaurant on Sixth Avenue. I asked what was troubling her. "I'll tell you," she said. "It's all those 'achs' and 'echs.' I come on and say, 'Ach, he's finally up,' or, 'Ach, you're finally here,' pick up a water pail and exit. What kind of a part is that?"

On paper, of course, the question seems valid enough, for

though Golde is obliged to react to everything that happens, she has no big moment of her own in the show. She appears in many numbers, but she shares them all; there is no song that is entirely hers. The anguish Marusha felt was not exclusive to her, as it turned out. At some point during rehearsal of each of the foreign *Fiddlers* I directed, the actress playing Golde voiced similar complaints either to me or to an interpreter. I remember a sudden and angry outburst in French from my Parisian Golde, Maria Murano—peppered with wild gesticulation and a series of ach and ech sounds. I needed no interpreter by then. I knew what was bothering her; it bothered them all.

Certainly *Fiddler on the Roof* is built around Tevye. He carries the burden of the show, and he gets most of the laughs. Even so, Golde provides balance and ballast. Tevye talks to God, but he listens to Golde. She is his antithesis, and though her lines are few compared with Tevye's, hers is an important presence in the show.

It's hard to convince an actress that her part is important when she obviously doesn't feel that it is, and the more Marusha was coached and cajoled, the more Golde seemed to be getting away from her. Jerry worried about her during rehearsals and was especially concerned after the Detroit opening, when spirits in general were down. Sometimes a director has to know when to do nothing, and in Marusha's case Jerry wisely let her alone for a few days. There was nothing more he could do or say to help her anyway. The show had always been rehearsed in bits and pieces—with less than a handful of run-throughs in New York—and perhaps she needed the continuity of performance repeated many times before she could come to grips with the part. Perhaps, too, she needed more time to build confidence in herself.

Whatever it was she lacked she finally found, and during a performance in the second week in Detroit, a magical turning point was reached. After the opening number, Marusha as Golde burst onstage and began ordering her daughters around with new strength and conviction, and as she talked of her ne'er-do-well husband we could see, beneath the surface irrita-

Maria Karnilova, as the long-suffering wife, in a moment of characteristic anger.

Friedman-Abeles, courtesy of Jacobson & Harmon

tion and frustration, the underlying love and need Golde had for Tevye.

Jerry and I looked at each other and hardly dared breathe for the rest of the act. I wanted to jump up and shout "She's got it!" for I felt very much like Colonel Pickering to Jerry's Professor Higgins, realizing that Eliza, at last, could properly describe that rain in Spain. By the end of the second act, in the reunion scene with Chava, Marusha was so moving that Jerry and I were close to bringing out handkerchiefs and weeping along with many of the people around us. Whatever had caused the breakthrough, it was clear that everything had clicked into place for Marusha, and from then on Golde lived.

For a director, facing an actor after such an occurrence is as delicate as tap dancing on tissue. Too little praise may lessen the achievement in the actor's eyes; too much praise may make it impossible for him to repeat what he has done or, at the other extreme, create complacency. Being Marusha's old friend, Jerry knew her responses very well. He commended the performance without being effusive but still giving her the confirmation she needed. The critic in Washington who later called her Golde "remarkable" helped reinforce her sense of security in the role. Her performance continued to grow in depth and power during the coming weeks.

Whether Zero appreciated her at the time we never knew, although it was clear enough that he considered her subordinate. From his standpoint the show was primarily Tevye's, and if he failed to recognize how important Marusha's performance was to his own success, that failure is forgivable. Few actors—particularly stars—are able to evaluate a performance from the audience's point of view, let alone from the director's. Almost all the Tevye-Golde teams I've worked with or heard about have had strong mutual differences, and the actors have ended up being antipathetic. The reason, Tom Abbott believes, is that the roles oppose each other all the time. And stage manager Jim Bronson has said facetiously that the antipathy is built right into Tevye's costume. "Once you put on the clothes," he said, "you hate Golde right away."

Yet it might well be the interdependence of the two roles that eventually becomes abrasive, for, after all, an actor likes to think that it is *his* work that is bringing a character to life onstage. Golde exists only because of Tevye; thus she is subordinate. But the interplay between them succeeds in showing a side of Tevye's nature that would not be apparent without her. The balance Joe Stein created for Tevye and Golde could probably be traced to the dawn of human relations, perhaps as far back as Adam and Eve.

6

The Perils of
Perfectionism

AFTER JERRY ROBBINS DECIDED to have me assist him in directing *Fiddler*, he gave me a warning that was disarming in its frankness: "I'm going to yell and scream at you a lot during rehearsals. I just want you to know that it won't be anything against you, but the deeper I get into a show the less patience I have with everything and everyone, particularly myself."

During the next weeks I was informed by several friends that, in effect, the experience would be a nightmare. Ming Cho Lee, Jerry's beleaguered set designer on *Mother Courage*, said nothing at all when I told him I would be assisting Jerry. He merely shook his head and looked at me with great compassion. And Conrad Bromberg, whom I had known since high school and who had played one of the sons in *Mother Courage*, held out absolutely no hope for the relationship. "You'll last two weeks," he declared. "Robbins is impossible."

No more encouraging, but certainly more helpful was a tip from Jerry's secretary, Edith Weissman. "When Jerry asks for something," she confided, "he doesn't want it today or tomorrow, he wants it yesterday." I watched the way Edith worked with Jerry and realized that she was his machinery, swift and efficient, and much of the time his memory as well. She would keep track of things he said he wanted and sometimes forgot to do, and whenever he appeared by her desk she was ready for him.

"You wanted me to remind you of this," she would say, pushing a letter or a memorandum into his hand. Or she might suggest that it was time to take care of some essential business, or she might even give him a choice: "Do you want to do this today—or that?" Because she was such a gifted administrator and his affairs were so capably managed, Jerry was free to function creatively in his own higgledy-piggledy way. Thus I knew from the beginning that I could help him most not only by being well organized but also by staying well ahead of him, anticipating his needs. It was not in his nature to be methodical. Tom Abbott and Ruth Mitchell, having worked with Jerry before, already knew what I was just learning.

Despite his warning, Jerry never did unleash his temper at me. Apparently he was much looser and more patient on *Fiddler* than he had been on previous shows. He did have his tense, black and grimly silent days—who doesn't? But his spirits were generally high, no doubt because he knew instinctively where he wanted to go with his material. This confidence never deserted him, not even during the Detroit "depression" when so many of us were losing faith.

It had been predicted by some that I would witness—or, worse, be involved in—violent scenes, but these never materialized. And though gossip columnists in New York were reporting that Jerry and Zero were quarreling furiously on the road, there was never even a mild confrontation. Tension existed, of course—some squinting of eyes and biting of lip on Jerry's part and behind-the-scenes carping and swearing on Zero's—but that was to be expected with two such wholly

opposite personalities being thrust together. It was only natural for Zero to want to experiment with funny bits, "shtick"
comedy and ad libs. And it was only right that Jerry would
often try and hold Zero back, so that Tevye the dairyman and
Aleichem the author wouldn't disappear from the stage.

The closest they came to open warfare was a silly and trivial
incident involving a wad of chewing gum. Jerry had urged
Zero not to chew gum during run-throughs, but Zero was in-
sistent. As the show began to take shape, the chewing became
more of an annoying distraction; it was hard to concentrate on
a dramatic scene with Zero in the middle of it, grinding his
jaws.

Late in rehearsals Jerry was conducting a kind of walk-
through of the first act, stopping only when absolutely necessary so he could get the feeling of it as a whole. Zero, as usual,
was aggressively chewing. Finally, Jerry called up to him,
"*Please* don't chew the gum." Zero removed it and stuck it
behind his ear. But during the next scene, whenever he was
turned upstage, he would pop the gum back in his mouth and
chew ferociously until just before he had a line; then he would
put the gum behind his ear, say his line, turn upstage and
repeat the whole process.

One look at Jerry was enough to know that Zero was danger-
ously overplaying his naughty-boy routine. It was as though
Zero wanted to provoke a battle, and I think Jerry sensed it.
We all watched and waited to see what he would do. But he
did nothing. He had no tolerance for insubordination, but he
obviously had some sense of proportion, even if Zero didn't.
To have an outburst over a wad of chewing gum seemed ridiculous and idiotic, and it never took place.

Jerry has an incredibly strong presence. A level of tension
exists when he is at work, an ever-present possibility of imminent explosion that usually helps keep actors on their toes
and under control. There is always the likelihood of a withering
public denunciation, if a performer isn't doing his utmost—
or if he is doing too much. During rehearsals in Detroit, one
of the children in the cast was characteristically attempting a

bit of scene-stealing in the wedding sequence. Calling her by name, Jerry's voice rang out from the darkness of the theatre, "You get offstage—where you belong!"

Jerry is not quick to offer praise, and each member of the company ultimately realized that not being picked on by Jerry was the equivalent of passing cum laude. And *no* criticism was the same as minimal praise, something few actors are used to. Nor was *I*, for that matter. In Detroit I began to feel, that for some reason, Jerry didn't like me. There was nothing overt, nothing he said or did, only an underlying coolness and brusqueness. We were together much of the time but seemed to have less and less to say. Sometimes as we sat waiting for actors to take the stage and begin rehearsing a scene, we would wait in silence. Gradually I began building up a case against myself. I was doing something wrong, I had disappointed him, he hated me, I was going to be bounced. I steeled myself against every possibility, giving prime consideration to the worst one, of course.

One night, returning to the hotel together after the nightly production meeting that followed a performance, we waited silently for the elevator to come. It was a silence I had grown to dread. Jerry's gaze focused on some distant point in time and space; mine pointed somewhere around my toes. The elevator came, we entered and continued to say nothing as the car ascended. But when it reached my floor and I started to step out, Jerry suddenly brought me into focus. "By the way," he said, "I want you to know I'm grateful for everything you've done. You're being very helpful." The doors closed automatically on my mumbled thank-yous. I felt like a child who had just been patted on the head, but the pats were welcome indeed. Thus passeth paranoia.

Months earlier, the first request Jerry had made of me was to organize his research. He wanted as much information as could be found on Jewish life and lore at the turn of the century, specifically the way people lived in the *shtetls* of Eastern Europe, the work they did, their professions. I scoured the secondhand bookstores on lower Fourth Avenue. I also visited

the library of the Yivo Institute on upper Fifth Avenue to bring
Jerry books and illustrations that would provide him with a
visual flavor of the times. This research gave him the basis for
attempting to communicate with Boris something of the scenic
values he wanted—and also to discuss with Patricia Zipprodt
the look he wanted her costumes to have (she was doing her
own—sometimes parallel—research, of course).

Tommy recalls viewing a couple of films with Boris and Pat
at Jerry's apartment on East 73rd Street. "One film was about
Chagall; the other was *Through Laughter and Tears,* and I had
to run that one again, stopping it every so often so a photog-
rapher who had come could shoot stills of whatever Jerry found
particularly interesting—costumes of the period of our show,
houses, a broken-down fence, old wooden stairs. These things
fascinated Jerry."

He was also fascinated by the symbol of a circle. Sheldon
recalls: "It was one of the first things he mentioned after agree-
ing to do the show. At that point he wasn't sure how he was
going to use the circle, but he felt it was important because it
was so common in folk-dance patterns." The circle became the
basis not only for the show's design, but also for the staging of
"Tradition," "To Life," the wedding celebration and the "Bottle Dance." At the end of the show the symbol was restated
most importantly during the exodus from Anatevka—when the
circle breaks up.

Jerry never wanted any of his actors in *Fiddler* to think of
themselves as singers or dancers. They were villagers, Anatevkans, either Jews or Russians (though in some cases doubling
as both). There were Yankel the grocer, Duvidel the seltzer
man, Yitzuk the streetsweeper, Hershel the potseller, Yussel the
hatmaker, Moishe the cobbler—names and professions created
so that each villager would have a sense of himself in the action.
Each had a purpose and a point of view toward everything that
happened.

Jerry expected the villagers to be consistently conscious of
their identities and was harshly critical if they behaved or
moved in a way that seemed out of character. As an exercise he

asked each of them to write an essay describing the character he played. The essays were turned in to me, and Jerry never asked to see them. He didn't need to; the exercise was for the actors' benefit. Writing the essays helped to heighten their self-awareness and the pride they were to feel at being Anatevkans.

Jerry had used an equally thorough approach to spectacularly good effect on *West Side Story*, for the fierce antipathy between the two rival street gangs was communicated powerfully to the audience. Tom Abbott, who had been in the original cast, recalls that Jerry very pointedly segregated the Jets and the Sharks during rehearsals. "He would say things like, 'Now the Sharks, this is your side of the stage, and the Jets, that is your side, and you stay there.' And the more each group could work as a unit, as a family, the better he seemed to like it. One day the Sharks came into rehearsal, and all of them—to a man—were wearing black leather wristbands. So the next day we Jets came in with rope belts. And we would always go out to lunch with members of our own gang. The two leaders, Ken LeRoy and Mickey Callan, helped keep the gangs apart, and Jerry encouraged it."

Tommy also recalls: "The bulletin board was not just for call sheets, with casting and rehearsal times; it had newspaper clippings of teen-age murders and gang fights. We were made aware of whom we were supposed to be at all times. Before each show, as I remember, we'd have a meeting of Jets and pick out which Shark we wanted to 'get' that night. Certain fight scenes were free-for-alls, not really set. We wouldn't go after the whole gang, mainly just one boy, and throughout the play we'd sort of keep bugging him." By Jerry's design, the fireworks that took place on that stage were only partly theatrical make-believe.

"I don't know how much regard Robbins has for himself as a director of actors," says Sheldon. "But just as he tried to make everything in *Fiddler* foolproof beforehand, I think he tried to get the best actors he could to take as much of the burden off himself as possible." He also tried to prepare them, as much as possible, for the demands of the show—not only before rehearsals began but in many instances before he had even cast them.

During the months of conducting auditions, Jerry invited actors he was considering seriously to come to his apartment, where they could talk with him—and read for him—in a relatively relaxed atmosphere. If, say, an actress was being considered for Tzeitel, he would have her read the two Tzeitel-Motel scenes with me; then he would discuss the scenes with her. He wanted to know what questions she might have—about the characters, about Jewish ghetto life in Russia, about anything that was unclear to her. He believed that by talking face to face with the actress he could instill a feeling for the period, for the character and for the character's emotional needs. Why, he might ask, did she think Tzeitel loved Motel? In what ways was she like Golde, her mother? How did she feel about her father, or about her sisters? Why was she more traditional in her outlook than either Hodel or Chava?

Jerry hoped that in finding answers to such questions the actress would be better equipped to grasp the part, but he was nearly always frustrated by his own good intentions. In almost every instance the actor in question read no better after the discussion than before. There might be a difference but not necessarily an improvement. More determined than ever, Jerry would probe the character in even greater detail. The actor would read again—and become more nervous, more self-conscious and less certain of himself. Other clues, additional insights, would follow; the actor would nod to each of them and then reread the scene or passage. In all likelihood his reading would be worse than when he started.

At the end of an afternoon of this, Jerry turned to me in exasperation. "What is it?" he asked. "I'm not getting from them what I should be getting, and these are the best of the people I'm seeing!"

I never volunteered opinions to Jerry; I waited until he asked me. "You're giving them good stuff," I said, "but I think you're telling them too much too quickly." If a director were to give me two or three suggestions during a reading, I said, I could absorb them and do what he wanted. But if he asked for seven or eight things, I could never come through. For some directors

I would simply have picked one or two of the things he'd requested. But if my director were *the* Jerome Robbins, I'd be so terrified that I would try to give him everything he asked for—and in doing so would be paralyzed and give him next to nothing.

"If I were you," I said, "I would tell them less." Perhaps he might give them two or three things to concentrate on, I suggested, to see how they responded—and then give them other things, if he wanted to see them again in a week or so.

Basically, Jerry agreed with me. He was well aware of his tendency to become mired in detail. Because he himself was searching for the various facets of each character, much of what he said to the actors was eventually more helpful to him than to them. He was also aware of his impatience, his desire for immediate "results." A dancer can usually do what a choreographer asks of him right on the spot—that is taken for granted —and Jerry has been both a dancer and a choreographer. But an actor must come to grips with complex feelings; he needs time to mull, to digest, to feel his way. Since becoming a director, Jerry had been trying to become more patient, and on *Fiddler* he succeeded admirably, as was verified by those who had worked with him on other, more traumatic occasions.

If Jerry Robbins is a warmer, less imperious person than George Abbott, he does share one trait with the veteran with whom he co-directed *Look, Ma, I'm Dancin'!* and *The Pajama Game*: single-mindedness. When Jerry is involved in a show, other people's problems and personal needs rarely enter his thinking. By being single-minded, he is constantly immersed in what he should be—the effects he wants to get on the stage.

Rehearsals for *Fiddler* were to begin Monday, June 1, 1964. I had just found a new apartment and was determined to move in before that date, knowing that with rehearsals seven days a week, I wouldn't have another chance for quite a while. On moving day, Saturday, May 30, I was up at 6 A.M. By noon I was in my new quarters, afloat on a sea of boxes and cartons that extended, wall to wall, across my living room. Jerry had asked that I call him at his country home in Sneden's Landing, once I was "settled," and after finding my telephone under a stack of books, I called him. I described the disarray that surrounded me and expressed the hope that things would be in some kind of order before Monday's workday.

"Oh," he said absently. "Well, look, in that case don't come up till around four today." And then he told me which bus to take so that he could meet me at 4:10. I mumbled that, sure, I'd be there, but I couldn't believe it! I looked around helplessly at the mess in the apartment and wondered what could be earthshaking enough to drag me up to Sneden's Landing on this of all days.

When I arrived, Jean Rosenthal was there, discussing the lighting of the show with Jerry. After she left, around six, Jerry and I had sandwiches while he talked about *Fiddler*. He wanted to discuss the characters—seemingly anxious to think out loud and test his own notions.

The reason for my visit soon became clear. By talking with me, he was trying to clarify and organize his approach to the characters—and to determine how, step by step, to proceed with his actors. If nothing else, I began to glimpse the depth of his insecurity. I think it's partly the fear of being found wanting, or shown to be inept, that drives even the most highly praised talents to work harder and harder.

I remember a party I attended not long after *The Sound of Music* had opened on Broadway. By chance, Richard Rodgers and I happened to be the only persons who chose a small den in which to eat our buffet supper. As we chatted about the theatre in general and his musicals in particular, his mood darkened when he spoke of the negative criticism he and Oscar Hammerstein had received for some of the more syrupy aspects of their latest show. He seemed to be drifting into a kind of bitter depression, and I made a vain attempt to bring him out of it. I reminded him of all the past triumphs he'd had with Hammerstein and with Larry Hart, and of the universal acclaim and respect he enjoyed, but he would have none of it. He just shook his head and stared down at his half-eaten food. "No," he said with a little sigh, "they take Gershwin seriously, but not me." No matter how brilliant one's talent, no matter how exalted the reputation, the insecurity seems to remain.

During a break one day, early in *Fiddler* rehearsals, I found Jerry in an exceptionally good mood. "How do you think it's going?" I asked. "Oh, I don't know," he said. "I don't think I'm doing anything good at all." Then he sort of chuckled. "Maybe this is the show where they'll find me out."

From the time Hal Prince had first become involved in *Fiddler*, he and Jerry had carried on a lively debate over the amount of rehearsal time that was needed. Jerry had insisted that he wouldn't consider doing the show unless he had eight weeks to rehearse, which he had been given on *West Side Story*.

"I was a little more reluctant with *Fiddler*," says Hal, "because I didn't think there was going to be that much dancing, and of course there wasn't." Hal felt that the financial burden of eight weeks would be too great, so he offered to compromise at five. But Jerry would not agree. His contracts are usually so complicated, and so demanding, that it takes a long time before they are ready for signing. Weeks passed. Even though the starting date for rehearsals was imminent, Jerry still hadn't signed—and could have withdrawn from the show if he had wanted to. But a new "compromise" was finally reached and he didn't have to.

"Sure, he got the eight weeks," says Hal, "but as it turned out, he didn't do any choreography until the next-to-the-last week. We had gone into the seventh week of rehearsals, and I was saying, 'When? *When?* You're still on the book! What you got out of this deal was six weeks' book rehearsal.' Then with the speed of lightning he did the opening number in about a day. The fact of the matter is that he was gun-shy of the dancing, and he was gun-shy for the best reasons. He didn't want 'dance pieces' in the show. The dancing had to grow out of parties or other totally naturalistic situations. He wanted no musical comedy dancing per se, which is why he was wary of it, and he was absolutely right.

"Jerry's no easy man to deal with, but when dealt with directly, frontally and honestly, it's a pleasure to do business

with him. The trouble is that we operate in a world where nobody delivers that way, nobody says *no* and nobody says *why*
—everyone just pussyfoots like crazy. Jerry and I get along
fine, really. I think we had one encounter on *Fiddler*. It was in
Detroit, and I remember the setting but not the issue—we were
standing on the stage behind a piece of scenery. It must have
had to do with my unwillingness to spend money for something.
The reason I remember it is that now that Ruthie Mitchell is
my associate, we have a standard joke. When I ask for something that costs money, she always says, 'If Jerry Robbins were
asking for it, would you give it to him?' I go home and think
about it and the next day I tell her, 'If Jerry Robbins were asking for it, yes, I'd give it to him,' or, 'No, I wouldn't.' That's our
rule of thumb."

Remembering that *Fiddler* was to have begun rehearsing in
January 1964—not June—I later tried to find out what caused
the delay. Only Hal could give a plausible reason: "It seems to
me that Jerry didn't think it would be ready then, so he ducked
it. That's why the delay, I think. Then a week or two before we were to go into rehearsal in June, he tried to duck it
again. He sent me a telegram that said, in effect, that he couldn't
go into rehearsal because the show wasn't ready. So I sent *him*
a telegram, saying that he should please send me a check for
$55,000, which was how much I was in the hole.

"Then his lawyer came to and said, 'Listen, what is this?' and
I said, 'It's nothing.' I was cooler than I'd ever been. I said: 'It's
no problem at all; we'll call it a day. Just send me a check for
$55,000 and there's no sweat.' He said, 'You can't—you're really
going to do that?,' and I said yes. Then he said, 'What's the implication?' I said, 'You know the implication as well as I do.
There's a verbal agreement here—an oral contract, perhaps he
hasn't signed yet—but he's let me go and lay out a lot of dough.
The show is ready, and I know Jerry. We've worked together
successfully and happily a long time. This is don't-go-near-the-
water.'

"I said that if I didn't get the money, I'd sue for it, and then
there was another exchange of telegrams. Finally, the lawyer

called and said Jerry was rehearsing with Tommy Abbott over on 47th Street, and asked if I'd go and have a talk with him. So I went over to the rehearsal hall, and Jerry said, 'You're not really going to make me go into rehearsal, are you?' I said, 'Yes, I really am.' And he said, 'Well, I just don't know what to do,' and it was all very bleak. He seemed genuinely upset.

"I understand it all much better now than I did at the time, and I'd probably be more compassionate about it—because the day before *Follies* went into rehearsal, I thought I had hepatitis, and I went to the doctor for a checkup. The next day I realized it was not an illness, just *naked fear*. That's all it was. I suddenly didn't know what I was going to do with that stage or those fifty people. I didn't think I knew what the style of the show was, after all that time, or what I was actually going to do."

Fiddler rehearsals began as scheduled at City Center on West 55th Street, with only the six young people at work: Tzeitel, Hodel, Chava and their suitors. Two entire weeks were devoted to them, which must have driven them nearly crazy, because there were only six short scenes to rehearse. The actors worked daily from eleven to seven. Although there were lunch breaks and hours spent at the piano, rehearsing songs, most of that time was given over to the dialogue scenes. With nothing else to distract him, and no other elements of the production to be concerned with at that point, Jerry was in paradise. He could rehearse to his heart's content. He never pre-blocked any scenes, preferring to extemporize with the actors on their feet. He also liked to improvise. "There never seemed to be any order to the day and certainly no plan," says stage manager Bob Currie. "Nobody knew what was going to happen next, but the *Fiddler* people must have known this was the way he operated. They were remarkably controlled."

"The first day of rehearsal," Hal recalls, "Jerry used a bookstore. They were rehearsing what it was like for a black person to buy books in a southern bookstore. The second day it was a concentration camp; Fyedka and Chava were playing Nazis and Jews."

I lost count of the hours we spent rehearsing the scene that takes place in the tailor shop when Chava and Fyedka first meet. Nor could I tally the variations Jerry imposed on the two actors. One day he made up a little tune for them to hum alternately—the idea being that Fyedka picks up the same melody Chava has been toying with. It was a nice idea, but, like others, it was thrown out.

Jerry then suggested that Chava be sorting bolts of cloth and Fyedka begin to help her, and when that was discarded they concentrated on Fyedka's book throughout the scene (which is the way it's been performed ever since). They reworked the scene repeatedly—endlessly, it seemed—and after four or five hours the actors were drained, but Jerry was fresh as a daisy. He was having a wonderful time!

When work with the script began, Bert Convy and Julia Migenes spent many long, maddening hours playing and replaying the scene that establishes the relationship between Perchik and Hodel. It was a difficult scene, for it contained a number of conflicting feelings—just how much of each feeling was part of the problem to be solved. "Stress the anger, not the attraction," Jerry asked at one point. Then he asked that the scene be played entirely for attraction and no anger. Later it occurred to him that the scene could be done more playfully, but then: "No, it's too sophisticated. Try playing it for innocence." Jerry was never satisfied. He kept experimenting, attempting new approaches, different combinations of expressed feelings.

"Jerry's way of directing book scenes is fascinating," says Hal, "because I've come to realize that it's the way most choreographer-directors work. It's what makes them do things over and over again in different ways. I mean, you have an actor come in the door from stage left; then you do the whole scene backwards and have him come in from stage right. To me it's just a mirror image of what you did before, and I don't see that the motivations or anything else are changed. But choreographers do this all the time with their dancers, and they continue to do it if they become directors. On *Fiddler* I saw Jerry have his actors do a scene literally fifteen different ways. Directors who are not choreographers tend not to work that way. They may repeat a scene until they get the texture right, and the motivations, but they don't keep changing directions; there's no temptation to do that. I saw this happen again when Michael Bennett and I were working on *Follies,* and I suspected that the reason it was happening was that, like Jerry, he had been a choreographer originally."

There was much less of a hassle in rehearsing the Tzeitel-Motel scenes—in part, I think, because Jerry had enormous respect for Joanna Merlin, whose Tzeitel was easily the best-acted part in the show during the first month of rehearsals. Except for the table-setting scene, where the characters urgently converse as they help prepare for the Sabbath meal (and where choreographic timing was essential), Jerry engaged in little trial-and-error with Joanna and Austin.

Rehearsals had been under way for little less than a week when Jerry and I had a quick corned-beef lunch around the corner at the Sixth Avenue Delicatessen. He was depressed and could barely eat, annoyed not only at Hodel, Perchik, Chava and Fyedka, but also at himself. He felt he wasn't getting the best from the foursome and that he was the one primarily at fault. I said that I felt the only problem was that he wanted "performances" immediately and wasn't giving the actors enough time to sink some roots and begin to breathe—and also that by doing each scene so many different ways each day, his people were getting punchy.

What I think was really troubling him was, that after several days, *he* couldn't decide how the scenes should be played. Then when inspiration struck and he had a completely new idea to impose on a scene, he wanted to see it *whole* right away, today not tomorrow.

Some actors are quicker than others, just as some infants walk earlier—it means nothing in terms of their eventual performance. Zero could instantly give Jerry everything that was asked of him—often even more—and Jerry wisely took advantage of it. He was relatively flexible with Zero, not only because Zero was the star but also because he was so incredibly creative.

The staging of "If I Were a Rich Man," Tevye's first solo number, was almost completely improvised by Zero. He asked if he could just play around with it, and as we watched he began moving about, shaking his fleshy body this way and that. Jerry helped him, suggesting the dips with his hands and how he might use one of the milk cans from his cart when referring to "a seat by the eastern wall" of the synagogue. But Jerry mostly let him use the gestures that seemed natural and right to him.

Sheldon remembers an equally important contribution Zero made to the effectiveness of that song, one for which he and Jerry Bock remain grateful. "We got scared of the serious ending," he says. "We wanted to drop it and make the whole song humorous, but he pleaded with us not to—to just let him do it the way it was, and he was right."

"Rich Man's" form had been inspired by a performance the composers had seen at a Hebrew Actors Union benefit held at a theatre on Second Avenue. "On the program," says Sheldon, "there was a mother and a daughter who sang a Hasidic song that was all 'boy-boy-boy-boy-boy-boy-boy-boy-boy' and in thirds and sixths most of the way through. Jerry Bock was so taken by it that he went home and wrote the music for 'Rich Man,' and when he put it on the tape for me, he just sang 'Boy-boy-boy-boy-boy-boy. . .' In order to preserve some of that flavor, I thought it would be marvelous if we could produce something that had those sounds in it. Then we got into rehearsals, and I found I couldn't do the sounds—those cantorial things—so I just wrote syllables, 'Digguh digguh deedle daidle . . . ,' which I'd heard when we went with Robbins to a Simchas Torah celebration in Williamsburg. Zero asked if I would mind if he didn't use what I'd written and kind of did it his own way. I said, 'Fine,' and what he did was wonderful."

At the end of a day's rehearsing, Zero would really be sweating and spent. For the most part he concentrated on what was asked of him, but nobody was more of a clock-watcher than he. His attitude was that he worked hard when he was supposed to, but not one second longer. And he didn't. One morning Jerry worked nonstop on the scene in which Tzeitel and Motel beg Tevye for consent to marry. They wear him down gradually, until finally he says, "Well, children, when shall we make the wedding?" Zero had been looking at his watch repeatedly. At exactly one o'clock, as Tzeitel and Motel stood waiting for Tevye's decision, Zero took a long pause and finally said, "Well, children . . . *lunch*," and walked right out of the room.

Everyone laughed. Jerry did too, but he would never have allowed anyone else in the company to get away with such prankishness. Zero was Zero, an overgrown Peck's Bad Boy, and something outrageous was always expected of him.

When *Fiddler* was approaching the end of its Washington run, one of Jerry's most pressing problems was simply to restrain Zero. Tevye was the rock on which the show was built; its architecture was in danger of collapse if Zero was permitted to become too broad. And he was always changing things—adding things, varying things, making things different. Thus there was concern that if he could not maintain a dependable measure of consistency through eight weeks of rehearsal and six and a half weeks on the road, how would he behave after six months on Broadway, or even a year?

Zero was very much on Jerry Robbins's mind when he left Washington for New York two days before the run actually ended. He told me he hoped to restore some measure of the objectivity he had lost. But that was not the only reason for his early departure.

Leonard Bernstein, Betty Comden and Adolph Green had been anxious to meet with him to discuss the musical adaptation of *The Skin of Our Teeth*, on which they were all collaborating. He spent the weekend huddling with them on an enterprise that ultimately became so problem-wrought and strife-torn that it had to be abandoned. Other Robbins projects would also fail to jell, despite the vast effort and creative energy that would be poured into them. Excluding the out-of-town doctoring on *A Funny Thing*—plus a few weeks helping to whip *Funny Girl* into shape for its New York opening—*Fiddler* would be Jerry's only musical to reach the Broadway stage throughout the 1960s.

7

"A Work of Art"
or "A Very-Near-Miss"?

THE WASHINGTON TRYOUT ended on a Saturday, and on Monday
morning *Fiddler* was rehearsing at the Ambassador Theatre on
New York's West 49th Street. Four blocks away the physical
production was being installed at the Imperial, where the show
would open eight days later. The show was close to being completely "frozen." All that remained was to decide the fate of
that much-rehearsed refugee sequence.

First order of business that Monday was a run-through of the
sequence for Hal and the authors. Afterward we all went to the
downstairs lounge to talk. Separately and privately, Jerry, Joe,
Jerry Bock and Sheldon had come to the same decision that
Hal announced: "Let's go with the second act we've got." There
was no dissension. The sequence didn't fit the show; its very size
and vivacity violated the mood of the second act, and it was too
obviously a concession to Broadway theatrics, or in Hal's words,

"It's the villagers gamboling on the green." As he saw it, if the small-scale second act was going to keep the show from being a popular success, then it was better to fail while being true to the spirit of the material than to try and jazz things up artificially.

Much later, almost everyone agreed that Bert Convy's hard-won song, "Now I Have Everything," also projected too much show-biz slickness, but the creative staff had been too close to the show in 1964 to realize it. According to Jerry Bock, "That was the equivalent of our second-act opening number, and we wanted an upsurge after the first-act finale, something bright and 'up' and positive." Even so, the song was cut from several foreign productions and from the film as well.

Both Gino Conforti and Ross Gifford were disappointed by the decision to kill the refugee sequence, as each was still hoping to play the part. But hardest hit of all were the girl dancers, for without that number their participation in the show was entirely minimal. What could be more frustrating for a Broadway dancer than to be cast in a Robbins show and end up with almost nothing to do!

After having performed the show for six and a half weeks out of town, the company faced its first New York audience five days before the opening. It was a Thursday afternoon, and the theatre was filled with friends, agents and performers in other Broadway shows—an audience similar to the one we had faced before leaving for Detroit. This time the reaction was considerably different, however. It was the best response *Fiddler* had ever received: roars of laughter, cheers, tears and thunderous applause.

Everyone was pleased—even a little shocked—because we knew the show had received some bad-mouthing in New York as a result of *Variety*'s Detroit review. But show-business audiences being unreliable barometers, we were all a little wary. We reminded ourselves again and again that their likes and dislikes could be very special, their reactions quite deceptive.

At the end I was standing at the back of the theatre, watching the curtain calls and listening to the applause. Tom Stone,

who had been a stage manager on *West Side Story,* was standing beside me, clapping ecstatically. "This is the greatest show
Jerry's *ever* done," he shouted to me over the din. Trying to
bring him back to earth, I yelled back, "You mean, outside of
West Side Story!" "Oh, no," he shot back, "*including* it."

Better than *West Side Story?* I hadn't known Jerry Robbins
or anyone connected with that show when I'd seen it, and
seeing it had been one of the most exciting theatrical experiences I'd ever had. Was this show in *that* league? This show,
which we had all been patching together and pooping around
with for weeks and months? It hardly seemed possible, and I
dismissed the thought entirely.

That night the first paying audience was as enthusiastic as
the invited audience had been, and the reaction was the same
at each of the remaining previews. Fears that though the show
had worked in Washington it might falter in New York evaporated quickly. The laughs were all in place, and so were the
tears; the handkerchiefs always came out as though on cue.
Broadway audiences were as consistent in their response as
the actors were now in their performances.

Like most directors, Jerry summoned the company to a rehearsal on the afternoon of the opening. Nothing much is ever
accomplished at these final calls, except that some of the actors'
anxieties can be alleviated by being given busywork.

The rehearsal was called for 2 P.M. A few of us were standing
outside the 46th Street stage entrance to the Imperial, chatting
as we waited for Jerry Robbins to arrive. Suddenly Zero was
spotted, making his way—but barely—down 46th Street toward
us. "Oh, my God," one of the girls cried, "he's smashed!" Indeed, Zero was weaving badly; at moments it seemed that he
might not reach us at all. No one even breathed as he weaved
abreast of us. Then suddenly he stopped, swung around on his
heels, let out a whoop of laughter, and marched soberly into
the theatre. It had been one of his "bits," and we were all
nervous enough to have fallen for it.

Jerry began the afternoon rehearsal by giving a few notes
from the final preview. By then there were not many to give.
After an hour or so of low-key fiddling and fussing, he dis-

missed the company—with no final speeches or snappy send-offs. I left through the front of the house, and when I reached the lobby I spied Sheldon standing in a long queue leading up to the box office. I couldn't imagine what he was doing there.

"Buying tickets," he said rather reasonably. I suggested that he might have just called the box office or asked someone in Hal's office to get the tickets for him, but he assured me he hadn't wanted to be pushy. As I left him I tried to envision Oscar Hammerstein II standing in line to buy tickets for *South Pacific,* but somehow I couldn't.

For years I was sure that nothing in the world could be as exciting or as glamorous as the Broadway opening of a musical. *Tenderloin's* hushed, doom-ridden premiere hadn't affected my fantasy, for *Fiddler* would assuredly be different. But I felt no excitement that September 22, only a sensation of unreality. I was tense and anxious, of course, for this night represented the culmination, the objective toward which everyone had been toiling for so many months. I was supposed to be back at the Imperial by 6:30 in case I was needed—which, now that I think of it, was ridiculous, for the one person who would be more helpless (and useless) than the director himself on opening night was the director's assistant! The show was even out of Jerry's hands now; the only thing he could do was wish everyone luck.

The curtain went up on time; the show played well; and though first-night audiences are notoriously cool, the reaction was warm and big. The turntable didn't falter, no traveler curtain got stuck, none of the boys dropped a wine bottle. There were no disasters, and Zero was at his absolute peak; his performance was entirely legitimate, extremely funny yet compelling and believable. Everyone, with the possible exception of Jerry Robbins, was convinced afterward that *Fiddler* was as good that night as it could possibly be.

Hal gave a company party at the Rainbow Room after the performance. Spirits were high, relief was great, the agony of the opening was over. "Jerry Robbins made a comment to me that night that I'll always remember," says Bob Currie. "He said it amazed him to look around and see all those people he'd been working with so long, because they seemed like human beings having a good time. Until then he'd thought of them only as obstacles in the way of his work."

After a while, in anticipation of the reviews, some tension began to cloud the party. At 12:15 A.M. word came that Walter Kerr's review in the *Herald Tribune* was not very good, and minutes later, when the *Trib* was brought in, the high spirits plummeted. Kerr led off by stating: "*Fiddler on the Roof* takes place in Anatevka, a village in Russia, and I think it might be an altogether charming musical if only the people of Anatevka did not pause every now and again to give their regards to Broadway, with remembrances to Herald Square."

Kerr clung to this theme through the body of his review, only to conclude: "Character is there to be touched. But *Fiddler on the Roof* dips below its own best possible level by touching character too casually, and sometimes soiling it with the lesser energies of easy quips, lyrics that stray too far from the land and occasional high-pressure outbursts that are merely marketable. The result is a very-near-miss, and I very much miss what it might have been."

Kerr was not the most influential of New York newspaper critics, the *Trib* (now defunct) lacking the prestige and circulation of the *New York Times*. But to most people, both in and out of the theatre, he was considered the most discerning critic, despite the fact that he had been erratic in his appreciation of musicals. He had found *West Side Story* "almost never emotionally affecting" and had seen little to like in Bock and Harnick's *She Loves Me*, which had charmed most reviewers and audiences. What was so dismaying about his criticism was his suggestion that the show was trying to be slick and commercial. Scrapping the refugee sequence had been the most recent example of a conscious desire on the creators' part *not* to give any "regards to Broadway."

"Kerr's review wasn't so much crushing as shocking," says Jerry Bock. "I could never have anticipated that kind of accusation, for the notion that we'd made so many concessions to the Broadway stage was beyond my comprehension. Maybe it takes the outsider to say that you were true here and here but not there, because I know how deeply involved we all were in trying to maintain continuity with the true fabric of the tales. It was a shock to learn that some of the things we wrote were out of key with other things; it would have been very difficult for us to have been the judge of that."

If the Kerr review had not come in first, its effect might not have been so devastating. But the thought—and the fear—that Kerr's words marked the beginning of a generally negative trend wrapped a cloak of melancholy around the Rainbow Room. Jerry Bock and Sheldon left immediately, and before long other people began drifting away, myself among them. The joy was gone; the bubbles had left the champagne; it seemed best to just go home.

"The thing *I* remember about that evening was that I wasn't interested in reading any reviews," says Hal. "This was because of my total confidence that the project was off and running. People came to me and said, 'Would you like to hear what the *Times* has to say?' and I said, 'No, I'll go on dancing.' I never doubted it for one second. I'll admit, though, that the entire time *Fiddler* was in rehearsal I was like a stranger to it. It was just so removed from me; the atmosphere of it, the whole genre, seemed foreign. And all the things they were going to put on their backs struck me as being ugly. The beauty of those people eluded me until much later. But the minute I saw the show on the stage in Detroit, the minute the sets and costumes were there and it was all of a piece, I knew that this was to be a very special theatrical experience."

The morning after the opening, in the *Daily News*, the tabloid that reached well over a million New Yorkers, John Chapman wrote that *Fiddler* is "one of the great works of the American musical theatre. It is darling, touching, beautiful, warm, funny and inspiring. It is a work of art." And Howard Taubman in the *Times* said that *Fiddler* "is filled with laughter and tenderness. It catches the essence of a moment in history with sentiment and radiance. Compounded of the familiar materials of the musical theater—popular song, vivid dance movement, comedy and emotion—it combines and transcends them to arrive at an integrated achievement of uncommon quality. The essential distinction of *Fiddler on the Roof* must be kept in mind even as one cavils at a point here or a detail there. For criticism of a work of this caliber, it must be remembered, is relative. If I wish that several of the musical numbers soared indigenously, if I find fault with a gesture that is Broadway rather than the world of Sholom Aleichem, if I deplore a conventional scene, it is because *Fiddler on the Roof* is so fine that it deserves counsels toward perfection."

In his concluding paragraph Taubman said: "Richness of flavor marks *Fiddler on the Roof*. Although it does not entirely eschew the stigmata of routine Broadway, it has an honest feeling for another place, time and people. And in Mr. Mostel's Tevye it has one of the most glowing creations in the history of the musical theater." As the day progressed and other critical voices were heard from, it seemed clear that the show was being hailed as eminently worth seeing and Zero's performance as a genuine treat.

I returned to the Imperial Theatre that afternoon, and what I saw there was certainly cheering: a long line stretching east on 45th Street, almost to Broadway. The line had formed early that morning and had grown so long that, despite the fact that the box office had three wickets, a man who joined the line at 10:20 did not actually have his tickets in hand until 1 P.M.

About $650,000 worth of tickets had been sold prior to *Fiddler*'s opening night—not only to individuals but to theatre parties as well. This was considered a very promising advance then, though not so staggering as the $1 million-plus accorded *The Sound of Music*, lured by the magic names of Mary Martin and Rodgers and Hammerstein.

Sure sign of success: outside the Imperial the day after the opening.

Courtesy of Jacobson & Harmon

Mostel might not have been Martin, and Jerry and Sheldon were a kilowatt or two less illustrious than Dick and Oscar, but *Fiddler* tickets were suddenly selling briskly. During the course of one memorable day, the Imperial box office took in $67,000, at that time a record for any Shubert house. As word of mouth began to spread and the magazine reviews came in, filled with adulation, there was good reason to believe *Variety*'s Broadway reviewer, Hobe Morrison, who on September 30 acclaimed *Fiddler on the Roof* as "the first blockbuster of the new season." In little over a week everyone realized that it was becoming a hit of legendary proportions.

In his book *Broadway*, published in 1970, Brooks Atkinson, the former dean of New York theatre critics, has some penetrating things to say about *Fiddler*. His opinion is not so much harsh as coldly detached, for that was always his way. As the *New York Times*'s theatrical tastemaker for thirty-five years, he was always the scrupulous journalist whose views were reasoned, astute, sometimes ascerbic, but never cluttered with sentiment or with speculation as to what a show might have been:

"When *Fiddler on the Roof* opened in 1964, just about everybody received it joyfully and especially liked the whirligig performing of Zero Mostel as a Russian Jewish peasant. But no one imagined that it would still be playing on Broadway six years later and long after Mr. Mostel had gone on to other parts. It became a staple item in the theater; it appealed to something fundamental in human nature. Since the music was commonplace and the libretto was routine, what was the quality that proved to be so durable? It must have been the folk genius of Sholom Aleichem, who created the folk hero, Tevye, the impoverished, devout dairyman who was forever arguing with God. . . . Unschooled, penniless, tormented in his own house, derided by his neighbors, Tevye was the perfect realist. He had a wholesome nature and no illusions.

There was nothing glamourous about *Fiddler on the Roof*. Tevye, his shrewish wife, his guileless daughters and his fellow townsmen lived in a slovenly Jewish community in Russia in 1905; they dressed in rags, torn coats and battered hats, and the men wore scraggly beards, and they all lived in a worn-out community—all of these things being the opposite of conventional showmanship. But there is a certain beauty in ugliness when enlightened artists deal with it. Boris Aronson's unadorned settings had vitality and aspiration; and Jerome Robbins . . . made a vivid composition out of the materials of the story. The sounds and the movement became the portrait of a civilized people—realism tempered with common sense, valor without heroics, and all of it suffused with warmth and humor. Beneath the facade of a big Broadway show, there was a core of human truth about some vigorous people."

Atkinson concludes his critique by suggesting: "When Sholom Aleichem settled in the Bronx in 1906, having fled the grisly Kishinev pogroms, no one could have imagined that in 1964 some audacious Broadway operators would invest $375,000 in a musical drama based on his fugitive stories and that New York theatergoers would buy $650,000 worth of tickets before the show opened. . . . Tevye would not have believed it. He would have expected God to compensate for commercial success with some awful and humiliating disaster."

That disaster didn't take place, but the show had a dangerous and potentially fatal problem during its first year: Zero Mostel. He had received the lion's share of huzzahs, and since he was the star he was considered *Fiddler's* life insurance, the key to the show's hoped-for longevity. Although it had been demonstrated in Washington that Zero and Tevye need not be inseparable and that the show could work without him, hit musicals are usually propelled by big-star performances. Thus it was assumed that *Fiddler* would prosper only as long as a major star like Zero headed the cast.

But once past the opening night, Zero began to let down. He felt free to step outside of Tevye—more and more often as the weeks and months went by—to become Zero the mimic, Zero the clown prince. "He was brilliant in the show, but he got bored," says Hal. On opening night he had been the best he would ever be. Soon afterward Tevye would become just another oddity out of Zero's bottomless bag of tricks.

8

Battling Zero

In the spring of 1965 *Fiddler on the Roof* was acclaimed by the Critics Circle as the best musical of the New York season, the first of many awards it would receive. The night after the announcement, Zero stormed into the Imperial Theatre, glowering and grumbling. Stage manager Bob Currie asked Zero if he was pleased by the kudos.

"You don't give awards to the show," Zero snarled. "You give awards to *me*." Whether joking or not—with Zero, who could tell?—the remark expressed a dark side of his nature that had become apparent as soon as *Fiddler's* success was assured. He would soon receive a Tony for his Tevye, but even so, he had come to feel that *he* was the show and the show would be much less without him. The press, as well as ticket buyers, had certainly given him reason to feel this way.

Variety had told its readers: "Add Zero Mostel to the tiny circle of great stars." The *Times* had proclaimed: "If Sholom Aleichem had known Zero Mostel, he would have chosen him, one is sure, for Tevye." Even Walter Kerr had conceded that Zero was "a delight." And *Newsweek* had effused: "He is the show's powerful heart and conquering soul . . . with him it is something not to be missed." He had waited years and endured painful reversals to achieve such recognition as was capped by a cover story (titled "Hail the Conquering Zero") that dominated *Newsweek* two weeks after its Zero-full review of *Fiddler.*

Born in Brooklyn's tenement-strewn Brownsville section, he was the son of a rabbi who was every bit as poor in means—and rich in spirit—as Tevye the dairyman. Zero recalls that though his parents "thought I was funny, in a peculiar sort of a way," they expected him to follow in his father's ordained and dedicated footsteps. What stopped him? According to Zero, his father. "He saved me once. My mother wanted me to be a rabbi. They were going to send me to Prague to study. . . . He asked me, 'Do you want to go?' I said, 'No.' He said, 'I'll put up a fight,' and he did."

What Zero wanted, after graduating City College and studying art at NYU, was to be a painter. He worked at it zealously —and has ever since. He would rather paint than do almost anything. ("I'm a painter who acts for a living," he says.) But the depression years were lean ones for artists, and though he was a painter and art teacher for the WPA, life was far from comfortable. His humor had always convulsed his friends. Now he was persuaded to branch out and try convulsing strangers as well, for maybe $3 or $5 a night. He performed his zany monologues in union halls and private clubs at first. But by the 1940s he was earning something akin to a high-living wage working in Broadway revues and in some of New York's sassier nightclubs.

He had begun making films, notably *Panic in the Streets* for Elia Kazan, when the repressive juggernaut of McCarthyism knocked his career completely off course. When an informer insisted that Zero had attended a Communist meeting that had taken place in Hollywood four years before he had actually gone there, the Red taint was strong enough to keep him on the blacklist, virtually unemployed, for years, until the cold shoulder accorded liberals began to thaw. It gave him a lot of time to paint.

In 1958 Zero the performer finally reappeared, not in films this time but Off-Broadway, as Leopold Bloom in Burgess Meredith's highly praised production of *Ulysses in Nighttown,* based on a section of the James Joyce novel. Suddenly Zero was a celebrity again. He became closely identified with Bloom, a part he has said he would like to play again. The tension that crackled through his hunched-over body made him Bloom to the life for admiring audiences, just as his snorting and raging projected the terrifying—yet hilarious—image of a man-turned-beast in *Rhinoceros* a few years later.

From that time on, he remained at odds with himself, a six-foot-tall fat boy who was never satisfied being just a comic, never quite refined enough to be a clown, but most comfortable hulking about as a buffoon. And the rowdier he became the happier he was, whether he was buttering his cuffs in a restaurant, wiping his mouth on a stranger's necktie, or emptying a glass of water on the floor during a TV talk show. Hal Prince remembers that during performances of *Fiddler,* "Zero started to wring his sleeve out over the orchestra pit after he got his sleeve stuck in the milk pail." The years of repression had left their mark; he was now irrepressible.

Fiddler on the Roof won nine Tony awards in 1965, providing medals for Mostel (musical star), Maria Karnilova (featured actress in a musical), Pat Zipprodt (costumer), Hal Prince (producer), Joe Stein (author), Bock and Harnick (composer and lyricist), and Jerry Robbins (director and choreographer). Jerry was the only one of this group to receive two of the coveted medals; he was also the only one not present at the ceremony.

None of the *Fiddler* recipients who preceded Zero Mostel to the podium that night so much as mentioned his name or acknowledged his contribution to the show's success. When

Zero's name was finally called and he mounted the stage, he said, "As long as nobody else has thanked me, *I* will thank me."

Admittedly, Zero carried *Fiddler,* for Tevye has the major share of lines and songs. If only in terms of physical energy expended, Zero more than earned his 10 percent of the gross per week (an amount that was sometimes upwards of $8,000). On opening night he certainly had been the "brilliantly resourceful and intelligent performer" that Richard Watts in the

A hardworking Zero Mostel rehearsing "Tradition" with village ladies.

Van Williams, courtesy of Jacobson & Harmon

New York Post said he was. But he soon became restless, and as the tidal wave of *Fiddler's* success rose to its crest, Zero began to slide. Much to the consternation of everyone, the show's creators as well as the actors who had to appear onstage with him, some troublesome antics began to corrupt his work.

At moments when his back was to the audience, he would make faces in an effort to break up the other actors. Or he would tug at the false beards of those who were no longer growing their own. One night, in a scene with one of the daughters, he pulled her close to him, according to direction, and then whispered, "Don't have garlic for dinner." The actress was so upset she could barely finish the scene. She left the stage in tears, and when Zero finally came off, she was waiting for him. "Don't ever do that to me again," she said. "I don't care *who* you are." And whenever Maria Karnilova's understudy, Helen Verbit, played Golde, she was fearful of the tricks Zero might play on her. During the wedding dance he often swung her so violently—and so precariously near the orchestra pit— that after one performance she cried, "I think he's trying to kill me!"

Tom Abbott, who had worked with Zero not only in *A Funny Thing*, but years before that in summer stock, says regretfully, "He made it impossible for anyone who was trying to concentrate and stay in character."

Tommy once went on for an ailing dancer who had a key role in the dream sequence. He was to carry the ghost of the butcher's late wife, Fruma-Sarah, on his shoulders (under a long, flowing costume), which gave her the appearance of being ten feet tall. As Tommy-Fruma approached Zero from upstage, Zero, whose back was to the audience, was just able to see Tommy's face behind Fruma's gown. He reached out and tried to poke two fingers in Tommy's eyes. Tommy bit him.

Among Zero's many talents is his ability to extend a single gesture into an elaborate pantomime routine. In scenes with Motel the tailor, he could "paint" hilarious pictures in space of Austin Pendleton. His face became a caricature of Austin's,

and he mocked the way the actor sputtered his lines. When
the audience responded, he would even imitate Austin's walk,
staggering about the stage, ankles inward. That was nothing,
though, compared to what he ultimately did in his first exchange with the constable.

In that scene the Russian officer warns Tevye that "a little
unofficial demonstration" against the Jews will soon take place.
Knowing that the "mischief" the constable refers to will be a
pogrom, Tevye thanks him, bowing obsequiously as the constable exits. Then he makes a good-bye-and-good-riddance
gesture toward the departing figure. It is a simple gesture
but a technically important one, because it cues the conductor
to start the music accompanying Tevye's next "conversation"
with God.

One night, before making this gesture, Zero reached up to
his own neck and maniacally began to "strangle" himself—
though obviously it was the constable he was pretending to
strangle. He got a big laugh. He strangled and strangled,
crossing his eyes for good measure; finally he made the gesture
that cued the orchestra. On subsequent nights he embellished
the routine even more. After strangling the constable, he
threw the body to the ground and kicked it—also to roars of
laughter. Eventually, the routine consisted of strangling the
constable, throwing the body down and kicking it, picking up
an imaginary shovel, digging an imaginary hole, picking up
the body and tossing it into the hole and then covering the
hole with dirt. There was applause as well as laughter; by this
time the good-riddance gesture marked the end of a one-min-
ute pantomime. Although it was indeed "brilliantly resource-
ful," it had nothing to do with the show. It didn't express
Tevye the humble Ukrainian milkman, but the inventive and
determinedly "conquering Zero."

When either of the stage managers tried to restrain him,
Zero insisted that none of his embellishments hurt anything.
Recalls Bob Currie: "He couldn't distinguish between those
moments when what he was doing was really genius and those
moments when it was just boorishness."

"And there were other things," Sheldon Harnick points out, "pieces of 'shtick.' And of course Zero denied doing shtick—he was above that, he said—which made it even more aggravating. Things got so bad that I was getting phone calls every week from people I'd given house seats to. They'd call and say 'Thank you for the house seats. The show is great, but did you know that Zero is doing such-and-such?' I'm sure 95 percent of the audience didn't care; they loved him, no matter what he did. But the 5 percent who did care were very unhappy about it."

"When we were working on the show," Sheldon remembers, "the question of using Yiddish words had come up, and we decided not to. I remember seeing too many nightclub comics, including Lenny Bruce, get cheap laughs by throwing in Jewish phrases. So we were careful. Then two months after we opened, in the scene where the Russian dancer bumps into Tevye, Zero let loose with a stream of Yiddish, under his breath. There was a big laugh from a section of the audience, but we were furious. We had worked so hard to keep that kind of thing out of the show. I spoke to Zero, but he wouldn't take it out for two weeks."

Says Joe Stein: "It was perfectly obvious that Zero had started to play *with* the show instead of playing the show. I did speak to him from time to time; he's not one to take criticism after he has a show under his belt. But that's Zero. He did give us an absolutely remarkable performance; at his best he's impossible to beat."

"Up to the opening," says Jerry Bock, "Zero was an exciting and remarkably spontaneous actor to be with—and marvelous to work with. He would feed *us,* improvising in such a way that we'd want to rush back and capture something he'd show us. But after the reviews came out, he took off as 'star.' His performance clearly changed; so did his attitude toward his confreres. When I saw how far he'd strayed, I went backstage after a matinee and tried as humorously and as affectionately as I could to tell him so. But he was very hard to talk to, very defensive, with a kind of 'count-your-blessings' attitude that he evidently conveyed to the cast as well."

"In order to be a comedian, you have to be extraordinarily sensitive," Zero once told an interviewer. "You have to have a censor in your mind as to what is comic and what isn't. There is a line, nondefinable but very much there. However, the whole purpose of comedy is to expose the bad air, to knock off the fakes. A guy who mugs or scuffs his shoes makes 'em laugh as a reflex, but the real comedian clears out pomposities . . . and stuffiness by making people laugh at them." And then, speaking about characterization, he told another questioner that "the more truthful it is, the better it is." The thoughts were sound, the words authoritative, but I wonder if he believed any of them.

Zero was fast and facile, his imagination always fertile, but from the beginning he'd had no sense of economy about his work. I remember that in the dream sequence his pantomimic reactions to the ghost were so broad, during out-of-town try-outs, and he clung to them so stubbornly, that Jerry had no choice but to take drastic action. He ordered Zero's follow-spot turned off when Fruma-Sarah entered, leaving the star of the show in darkness. Zero continued his mugging and a busy routine with his nightgown, but few in the audience could see him —or laugh at him—and the lyrics being sung by the ghost could at last be heard.

A director is contractually expected to keep an eye on his show after it has opened, if and when he is in town, to help keep it fresh and alive and solidly on its feet. But Jerry Robbins felt compelled to stay away from the theatre, so appalled was he by Zero's antics. "I don't recall Jerry's coming to *Fiddler* more than once or twice that first year," says Tommy. "And even then it wasn't for a complete performance." Zero well knew how displeased Jerry was, but he wouldn't give up the shtick.

"I think Zero had a nine-month contract with the show," says Jerry Bock. "And when the contract came up for renewal, he evidently asked some extraordinary terms. Why not? He thought, and we did too, that he was carrying the show. I remember Hal coming to us to say that he didn't think he was going to meet Zero's terms, and asking how we felt about it. That was perhaps the first time we had to assess *Fiddler*'s success—was it the show or was it Zero? We really didn't know, but we all said, 'Okay, let's find someone else.' Before he left, Zero said he would give the show a few weeks, a month or two at most. He was dead serious, and at that point, as far as we were concerned, he could have been dead right."

Zero's departure was unmourned by most of his fellow actors —until some days later when they realized how much less of a show they now had with Luther Adler, Zero's replacement. Adler had always been a fine actor—at times a distinguished one—but he had few qualifications for playing Tevye. The role's lightness evaded him; as far as the cast was concerned, he seemed determined to make it heavy.

Adler first played the role in January 1965, when Zero took a two-week vacation; he returned in June when Zero's contract expired. The stage managers had blocked him through his scenes initially; then Jerry Robbins was to rehearse him intensively. "But that didn't work out," says Tommy. "Jerry worked with him about two days but was getting nowhere. Adler seemed determined to make it so serious—like 'Tales from the Bible' or something. Jerry came to Adler's opening night, and as the show progressed he just sank in his seat. It was so ponderous and slow."

"I was disappointed with Luther only in the first part of the show," says Sheldon, "only in what I consider the musical comedy moments. For me, his performance got better and better as the show went on, and by the end of it I loved him."

"I liked Adler," says Jerry Bock, "even though the difference between him and Zero was enormous. What Luther did was give us the transitional replacement that allowed for other replacements. He bridged a gap in some crazy way. I liked some of his second act, but I felt Herschel Bernardi was better."

For years I wondered why Jack Gilford had never been asked to play Tevye. Here was an actor, I felt, who could have won all the laughs and melted the hearts of the audience as well—a gifted and capable performer. It was Sheldon who told me that Gilford *had* been auditioned and why he had not been cast. "We all loved Jack's work," he said, "but interestingly enough, we weren't sure he could play anger. At one of his readings, whenever he had angry words to say, he would take a step backward, as though he was really backing away from that kind of emotion. I talked with Jack's wife about it afterward, and she said she couldn't understand it. 'Jack can be very angry; he's got a temper,' she assured me. But onstage he didn't show it."

When negotiations with Zero first began to bog down, says Hal, "I remember Jerry Robbins saying right off the bat, 'Let Zero go. Why not let Paul Lipson play it?' But I didn't have the guts for that. We made that trip in stages." Luther Adler was the first stage. He was to play the role on Broadway long enough to become at least partly identified with it and then head the national company, which was soon to tour the country—and would eventually make the tour a second time.

I remember Joanna Merlin telling me then, "I never thought I'd be saying I wish Zero were back, but that's the way I feel." To the surprise of everyone connected with the show, and to Zero, too, I imagine, the public did not seem to feel this way. *Fiddler on the Roof* continued to play to packed houses not only with Adler and then Bernardi, but also with Harry Goz, Jerry Jarrett, and, of course, Paul Lipson. In mid-1971 Paul played his 1,500th Tevye; he had performed that part—on tour and on Broadway—more times than any other actor in the world.

On March 31, 1971, *Fiddler's* Broadway run exceeded that of *My Fair Lady*, and on July 21, with its 2,845th performance in New York, it overtook the champion, *Hello, Dolly!*, to become the longest-running Broadway musical in history. Only two nonmusicals, *Life With Father* with 3,224 performances, and *Tobacco Road* with 3,182, have run longer than *Fiddler*. The show had been a triumph for Zero Mostel, but it proved to have no less magical attraction without him than with him. It can be argued whether *Fiddler* was Jerry Robbins's greatest show, but it was certainly his greatest popular success.

9

"No Bagels in Tel Aviv?"

DURING *Fiddler's* first year on Broadway, Hal Prince received numerous bids from producers who wanted to have the show staged abroad. Many wanted exact re-creations of the Broadway production, complete with Boris Aronson's sets, Pat Zipprodt's costumes, and Robbins's staging and choreography —all of which were possible, of course, even though Jerry himself was uninterested in restaging the show. Since Tommy and I had assisted Jerry, we were the logical ones to be asked to transfer Jerry's work to some of the foreign locales.

The first overseas bid to be accepted was from producer Giora Godik in Tel Aviv, a likely place to stage a musical that concludes with Jewish peasants being exiled and dispersed from the land of their birth. If any foreign musical would be meaningful to Israelis, it seemed certain that *Fiddler* would be the one. As moving as the final scene had been for American audiences—when Yente says that even if she has to walk or crawl, she's going to the Holy Land—we were sure it would have a shattering effect in Israel itself, where theatre audiences would be filled with immigrants like Yente, or their descendants. And since the creators of *Fiddler* had all been Jewish, it was appropriate that the first foreign production was to be in Israel. In my case, it greatly pleased my grandmother that I would actually celebrate a Passover in the Promised Land.

Tommy and I were to fly to the Holy Land in April 1965 and begin working with an all-Israeli cast. I was terribly excited, but I also felt some trepidation. I didn't speak Hebrew and had received little religious training as a child. I began to bone up once again on everything Jewish that related to the show—the ritual, the folklore, the superstition and especially the Aleichem stories. I "prepped" myself so I could answer any questions my actors might have about life in the *shtetls* of Eastern Europe, or about the degree or the effect of religious worship at the turn of the century.

I was determined to keep a step or two ahead of my actors, and I wanted to be able to justify every aspect of the show— every gesture and every movement—with facts from Jewish history. I assumed that the actors would know everything, that they would be serious-minded, religious people for whom *tradition* would not be just the name of a song. I boarded the plane to the Holy Land well armed to face a cast full of rabbis.

I arrived in Tel Aviv on April 11 and was greeted by bright springtime weather that was more like early summer: sunny and warm without yet being uncomfortably hot. Apartments were found for me and for Tom, in both cases near beautiful beaches. It was a temptation we often couldn't resist to break rehearsals early and sneak in some sunbathing and swimming.

For such a small and comparatively new country, Israel had an astonishing amount of theatrical activity, most of it centered in Tel Aviv. Not only the well-known permanent companies, like the Habimah, but smaller experimental groups flourished as well. Pinter, Albee, Osborne and Beckett were being performed—and argued heatedly at Kesset, the Joe Allen's of Tel

Aviv's theatre community. Listening to vehement arguments at Kesset (Israelis seemed to be passionately opinionated about almost everything), I was even able to pick out from all the unintelligible Hebrew the unmistakably familiar name "Neil Simon."

Despite heavy competition, most theatres played to full houses—even movie theatres. My producer's office had to reserve seats in advance if Tommy or I had time off and wanted to see a film. All this was before television arrived in Israel; plays and movies filled an important need in keeping Israelis in touch with the "outside," the somewhat remote Western world. Even a flight to nearby Greece or Italy was a luxury most Israelis could not afford.

Tel Aviv's abundant theatrical activity was not necessarily a boon to *Fiddler*. Most of the country's better actors were contracted to permanent companies, and there were relatively few first-rate free-lance actors to choose from. (A similar situation exists in Amsterdam, Vienna and other European cities.) Giora Godik was one of the few independent commercial producers in Israel. His production of *My Fair Lady* had been a phenomenon—the first large-scale musical to be performed by an Israeli cast. (Other musicals, such as the Godik-sponsored *West Side Story*, had toured Israel with American or European casts.) It was such a huge success, in fact, that Godik had come to be known as the "Israeli David Merrick" (there are similarities in personality, too). Godik had taken a backward step with his second musical, *How To Succeed in Business Without Really Trying*, which had proved hopelessly American. Backstabbing on Madison Avenue was totally alien to the Israeli experience —not only unfunny but meaningless—and the production folded quickly. With *Fiddler* Godik hoped to restore his prestige and replenish his bank account.

Because this first remounting was so important, Tommy and I were not the only ones from the original production to become involved. Boris Aronson came to Tel Aviv to oversee construction of the sets, as did Fred Feller, who had built the original sets and turntable. Ruth Mitchell arrived in time for the technical rehearsals and helped the resident stage managers organize *Fiddler*'s complex backstage world. And Joe Stein arrived during final rehearsals so he could make any text changes that might be needed.

Fiddler was to be presented at the cavernous Alhambra Theater, oddly located in drab, impoverished Jaffa, an adjunct of Tel Aviv. Although only ten minutes from the immaculate and bustling "downtown" Tel Aviv, Jaffa was a depressing contrast. The many abandoned shells of buildings told of an area that had not been rebuilt after suffering punishing air raids. The contrast was similar to that provided by the gray and shabby hopelessness of East Berlin versus the heady rhythms of West Berlin's Kurfürstendamm.

By the time I arrived in Tel Aviv, Godik and his associate producer, Yoram Kaniuk, had auditioned most of the available actors, and candidates for each role had been narrowed down to two or three, so that I would have a choice—an effective system that was later repeated successfully with the Paris production. What surprised me most at the auditions was the attitude of many of the actors. Several informed us, through our interpreters, that they wouldn't consider such secondary roles as the butcher or the innkeeper; it was to be Tevye or nothing. (In New York, by contrast, we could fill a theatre with character men desperately eager to play Lazar Wolf *or* Reb Mordcha.) The attitude was primarily due to the fact that Tel Aviv was such an "actors' market," with so many shows being performed. An actor knew that if he didn't get a part in Godik's show, he would land a job elsewhere quickly enough.

The name Chaim Topol was never mentioned as a possible candidate for Tevye. Two well-known actors, Shmuel Rudensky and Shraga Friedman, had been seriously considered, but they were committed to other projects. (Rudensky later played some performances in Tel Aviv and was Tevye in the long-running West German production.) The only conceivable candidate was Bomba J. Zur, a roly-poly comedian who had won much acclaim for his Mr. Doolittle in Godik's *My Fair Lady*. To play opposite Bomba we cast Lya Dulitzkaya, a warm and gifted

Tevye and the fiddler in their only scene alone, meeting on the street outside the inn; left to right, *Yaacov Maman and Bomba J. Zur. Tel Aviv.*

actress and singer who has since earned the distinction of having played Golde in four languages: Hebrew and Yiddish (Israel), German (Austria) and English (South Africa).

The last thing I expected to find in Israel was race prejudice of any kind, but Tommy and I bumped into it squarely during auditions. It seems that there is a caste system that places European Jews on a higher plane than Oriental or Eastern Jews, who appeared more dark-skinned and Arabic. The Asiatic Jews tended to live together in unofficially segregated parts of Tel Aviv and filled most of the city's more menial jobs.

As we had expected, there were few talented dancers to

choose from in Tel Aviv. But among the best of them was Zeev
Melichi, whose coloring, we noted, was a shade darker than that
of the other candidates. When Tommy said that he wanted to
cast Zeev, Godik refused. Both of us insisted at that point, and
Godik reluctantly explained that Zeev was a Yemenite and
wouldn't fit in with the rest of the company. We refused to back
down, and Godik was either too embarrassed or afraid that the
situation would become a cause célèbre, so he finally agreed.
For good measure we cast one Yaacov Maman, also a Yemenite,
in the role of the fiddler.

Language problems arose soon after casting had begun.
As neither Tommy, the company gentile, nor I spoke Hebrew,
Godik hired Amnon Kabatchnik to assist us. Amnon was an
Israeli-born director who had worked in New York and was
fluent in English.

I knew the show so well by this time that at auditions, even
though I couldn't understand the Hebrew words, my mind automatically followed in English whatever was being said—a
process I later repeated where Dutch and French were involved.
I was interested in having a girl named Aliza Fischer play
Tzeitel. I could tell by her presence and the feelings she expressed—as I followed her reading with my silent instant-trans-
lation—that she would be fine in the role. But Amnon told me
what I couldn't hear myself. She spoke Hebrew with an American accent, because she was from the States. We cast Aliza in
the chorus but could give her no lines to speak. I subsequently
learned that she was the sister of my lawyer in New York.

As auditions proceeded, I became aware that something was
wrong with my instant-translating. Speeches were sounding in-
ordinately long, even making allowances for normal language
differences and translation problems. Moreover, the very
rhythm of many speeches seemed different and wrong. I asked
Amnon to go through both my English script and his Hebrew
version to see if there were important discrepancies. He discovered, to our mutual horror, that the translator had added
quite a bit of his own material—jokes and embellishments that
were neither called for nor very good.

I told Godik that I was responsible to Jerome Robbins and

Joseph Stein to reproduce their show, and that the original script would have to be restored. He agreed, but even so there was scarcely time to do it. Rehearsals were to begin in a few days, and our daytime hours were still consumed by the auditioning of singers and dancers. Yet the restoration would have to be finished so that new scripts could be duplicated in time to distribute to the actors at the first rehearsal.

There followed a series of exhausting nightly meetings that lasted into the early morning. The meetings took place either at Tommy's apartment or mine, and the procedure we followed —the only one that seemed feasible—was agonizingly slow. Tommy or I would read a line in English. Amnon or Yoram Kaniuk would give us a literal translation of the equivalent Hebrew line. We would then point out what was wrong with the line, in meaning or emphasis. Amnon and Yoram would argue between themselves as to how our English words could be put into the best possible Hebrew. Some nights we completed two or three scenes, other nights only one. It often took as long as twenty laborious minutes to discuss, dissect and debate a single line of a speech. Somehow, despite the snail's pace of our progress, the revision was completed in time.

Seared by this experience, I had the lyrics examined carefully and was relieved to find that Sheldon's ideas had been well transcribed. The limitations imposed by the musical notes and the meter had been difficult enough for the adapter to accommodate, let alone strain to add fillips of his own. The language difference, and the presence of either more or fewer syllables in a line or phrase, made some deviation necessary, but none of it violated the spirit of Sheldon's intentions. Thus, to fit the melodic pattern of the song without sacrificing any of its sentiments, "If I Were a Rich Man" became "If I Were a Rothschild," a prophetic change, considering the subject of the seventh Bock and Harnick musical, little more than five years later.

Almost as maddening as rewriting the script were the weekly production meetings involving the various technical departments. What should have been one-hour sessions often dragged on for three or four hours. After every two or three sentences in

Hebrew or English, translations would have to be made in other languages so that everyone would know what was being planned or decided. Izhak Graziani, our musical director, understood only Hebrew and Italian. The wig lady communicated only in German. The shoe man had to have everything translated into Polish, which Boris Aronson fortunately was able to do. It was like a nightmare version of a United Nations committee meeting.

Even at rehearsals, communication was often crazily backwards. I would arrive in the morning and greet an actor with "Shalom," and he would answer "Good morning." And when greeting our Hodel, Etty Grottes, I would try and remember to say "Buenos días," as our only common language was my limited knowledge of Spanish.

We had six weeks to rehearse *Fiddler,* and though this might seem an unusually long time, we needed every day of it, considering not only the language difficulties that slowed us down but a very green technical staff and crew. Unlike the crisp efficiency of Broadway, where time is money and neither is likely to be wasted, much time was lost in Tel Aviv not only because of lack of experience on the part of persons involved but lack of discipline as well. Those of us who had come from New York had to compensate for the lack of experience, but Tommy and I were determined to instill a sense of discipline in the actors and crew.

When we announced the rehearsal schedule—10 A.M. to 6 P.M. each day, with an hour off for lunch—the company thought we were madmen. Most had never rehearsed more than two or three hours a day on any show. Because all public transportation stopped at sundown on the Sabbath eve, we had to end Friday rehearsals at 3 P.M. and of course were forbidden to rehearse on Saturdays. Sunday was the first workday of a new week, like Monday in the States, and this took a bit of getting used to. We were not allowed to rehearse on Israeli Independence Day—which fell on May 6 that year—and at a time when we could ill afford to take a day off. I argued that American actors often perform and rehearse on the Fourth of July, but my pleas fell on deaf ears—so I had an extra day at the beach.

One minor frustration of life in Tel Aviv was that every store, restaurant, movie house and legitimate theatre was closed from Friday evening until sundown Saturday. As a then-heavy smoker, I learned the hard way to lay in a supply of cigarettes before the Sabbath shutdown.

Decorum at rehearsals, or simply keeping order, was always a definite problem, Israeli actors being irrepressibly chatty. "*Sheket!*" is a word Tommy and I became familiar with quickly; it means "Shut up!" I also invoked one declaration that was guaranteed to terrify any and all: "Jerome Robbins is due any day." Although Jerry had notified me that he wouldn't be able to visit Tel Aviv, threat of his imminent arrival was too valuable and effective a tool not to be used from time to time. Jerry's reputation as a brilliant choreographer, and as a frighteningly demanding genius, is apparently known by actors around the world, so Tommy and I continually reminded the company that Robbins was likely to appear at any time, without any advance notice. The reminder always had a sobering effect, and for a time the chattering would diminish.

We had other specific and very annoying problems relating to discipline. For example, a few of the men in the company were reluctant to grow beards. We warned them that they would be fired if they didn't, a threat that worked in all but one case. We had to fire a dancer who shaved his beard because he said it was interfering with his social life.

In Tel Aviv as in other foreign cities, Tommy had an especially difficult time getting the strength and vitality from his dancers that Jerry had always insisted upon. Tommy remembered how demanding Jerry had been in rehearsal—just when it seemed the dancers were giving everything they could, he wanted more. And in rehearsing the wedding dance, when the boys seemed to be giving the maximum amount of vitality to their work, every bit of strength they had to their stomping, Jerry would ask for twice as much. He said it wasn't good enough, even when they felt they couldn't possibly do any better, but his demand was not unwarranted.

Sheldon Harnick says: "I remember when Harold Clurman reviewed the show. He liked it, but he said the dancing surprised him because he didn't associate Jewish dancing with such violence. And I wanted to write and urge him to go to those weddings at the Ansonia, because I remember a circle of Hasidim stamping on the floor until I thought the floor would come down."

"It was an interesting discovery to find out how physical and aggressive these people were," says Jerry Bock. "It helped us in a way, at least subliminally, for we realized that these were not faint valentines of years gone by. The tradition was still here today, and in a very vibrant and vital sense."

In Israel, to my surprise, another tradition was being upheld. There was a female villager in our cast who had no qualifications at all other than the fact that she was somebody's girl friend. We never knew who that somebody was, but at auditions we were told that she *would* be cast, and we got the message. Tommy and I tried to conceal her far upstage in the crowd scenes, but her height made it difficult to hide her. Apparently eager for a movie talent scout to spot her in the show, she tried to get away with wearing gaudy makeup and a fancy hair style. As makeup was not used by anyone in *Fiddler*, except for the two ghosts or for purposes of aging, we gave the young lady her choice: Either take off the makeup and hairpieces or remain offstage. After three nights of standing forlornly in the wings, beautifully made up and coiffed but with nowhere to go, she gave up and decided to become a Jewish peasant after all.

As to my earlier fears that my Israeli cast would be composed of forty-four Talmudic scholars, I was amused to realize that I had to remind my actors constantly to kiss the mezuzah whenever they entered or left the tailor shop or visited Tevye's home. And they needed constant policing to make sure they first touched the mezuzah with their fingertips and then brought those fingers to their lips, not vice versa. The Israelis were more forgetful of Jewish ritual than any other cast I worked with.

The inexperience of our technical staff and crew proved

more, rather than less, of a problem as time passed and our opening date came nearer. The first technical rehearsal, even with Ruth Mitchell's steady helmsmanship, was a chaotic mess. Much of the scenery was still unfinished; the lights were improperly focused; only some of the dancers had shoes; and only half the props had actually been acquired. During the street scene in Act One, the bagel man appeared carrying a naked stick on which a number of bagels was supposed to be stacked. I was thoroughly exasperated by then, and I yelled up to the stage, "So where are the bagels?" The prop man was summoned, and the question was repeated. "We can't find any," he shrugged. "*No bagels in Tel Aviv?*" I shouted. He shrugged again, as unconcerned as a waiter at the old Lindy's, and left the stage.

We had a week of public previews, unheard of in Tel Aviv but certainly needed in *Fiddler*'s case, to iron out the technical wrinkles. Ruth's presence backstage was enormously helpful, but on June 2, five days before the opening, we lost her services. She returned to her hotel after a performance had ended. As she was picking up her key at the front desk, she spotted her luggage stacked neatly in a corner. She inquired and was told that she had been moved out of her room. Godik, it seemed, had misinformed the hotel about the length of her stay, and her room had been rebooked. Ruth was outraged, but the hotel manager was indifferent. He was even indifferent to the fact that it was then the middle of the night. "Haven't you at least arranged for me to move to another hotel?" she asked, but the manager said no. Ruth picked up her bags, got into a cab, drove immediately to the airport and left Israel.

Throughout our entire rehearsal period we had willingly endured the continuous pounding and banging made by workmen installing an elaborate air-conditioning system in the theatre. The noise drove us crazy, but the results, we were assured, would at least be worthy of our suffering. Opening night was fiercely hot, and as we might have expected, after all those weeks of mayhem, the cooling system broke down. Fortunately, *Fiddler*'s particular magic cut through the steamy circumstances, captivating a distinguished audience that included Israeli cabinet members and their wives and the late Premier Levi Eshkol.

"My most vivid memory is of the night before the opening," says Joe Stein. "It was a free preview for the army, and the place was filled with soldiers. There had just been a rather serious border incident, so they had a captain in the box office with an open mike to headquarters—in case our audience was needed at the front. They were Sabras, real tough Israeli kids who don't give a damn about the old folks. I was very nervous about them, but they turned out to be a marvelous audience."

Fiddler was an immediate hit, and many Israelis who themselves or whose forebears had survived the Russian pogroms and the Nazi holocaust came to the Alhambra Theater two and even three times. The show played there a year and a half, went on tour to Haifa and Jerusalem and then returned to Tel Aviv to continue the run in Yiddish, with as many of the original actors as could speak the language. This time Godik had little success. Hebrew is Israel's official language—Yiddish is frowned upon and slowly dying out—and the new version lasted only a few weeks.

"Matchmaker, Matchmaker." Tzeitel (Atalia Cahana) singing to Hodel (Etty Grottes), with Chava (Tirza Arbel) looking on. Tel Aviv production.

Mula & Haramaty

10

"But It Won't Work Here"

IT SHOULD HAVE surprised few people that *Fiddler* was a success in Israel. But before rehearsals began on each of the three European productions I staged, there were glum looks and dire predictions that this time, certainly, the show wouldn't work.

I loved Amsterdam from the moment I arrived. With its beautiful canals and lovingly preserved old buildings, it had an atmosphere that seemed wonderfully peaceful compared with the fast pace and day-to-day trauma of life in New York City. Amsterdam seemed to have all the advantages of a major city but few of the problems. And for a nonlinguist like myself, it was pleasant to be in a country where people not only understood English but were eager to speak it, to polish their use of this important second language. As one friend put it, "We can't expect to be able to travel around the world and speak *Dutch* to anyone." It was such a pleasure being in Amsterdam that I returned two years later to stage another musical at the same Theatre Carré for the same producer, Paul Kijzer.

The man who was assigned as my dialogue director on *Fiddler*—and who acted as my interpreter when I had to communicate with a few of the older, non-English-speaking actors —was a Dutch actor, Jan Teulings, well known as Inspector Maigret on television. We had dinner my first night in Amsterdam, and as we talked about the show I found him strangely condescending. I tried to spark some enthusiasm in him, but to no avail. Finally he said, "You know, this show will not be successful here." "Oh," I replied, trying not to bristle, "why is that?" "Well, for one thing," he said, smiling, "there are not many Jews left here. Also, there is little in the Dutch character to make them identify with the people of Anatevka."

I was taken aback and more than a little annoyed. It was possible, I thought, that he might be right. But if so, what could I do about it? I was there and my work was cut out for me. There was no alternative but to stage the show as best I could and hope that audiences would be receptive.

During the next weeks I was informed repeatedly that most American musicals, with the inevitable exception of *My Fair Lady*, had failed in Amsterdam. From the first preview of *Anatevka* (as the show was called there), Dutch audiences responded exactly as audiences in the States and in Israel had. They loved the show, as did the critics. "You have to see *Anatevka* at least twice to see all the beauty," said *De Telegraaf*, and a leading Catholic newspaper, *Volksrant*, proclaimed: "*Anatevka* is a terrific feast. There is nothing, absolutely nothing, that we can criticize in this show. It will be a triumph all over the country." The critic was right, for the production remained at the Carré a full year and then successfully toured Rotterdam, The Hague and other Dutch cities.

Overleaf, top: "*So what would have been so terrible if I had a small fortune?*" Lex Goudsmit, who played Tevye in the Amsterdam production.

Overleaf, bottom: *The ghost appears.* Left to right: *Lex Goudsmit (Tevye), Enny Mols-de Leeuwe (Golde), Carry Tefsen (Fruma-Sarah).*

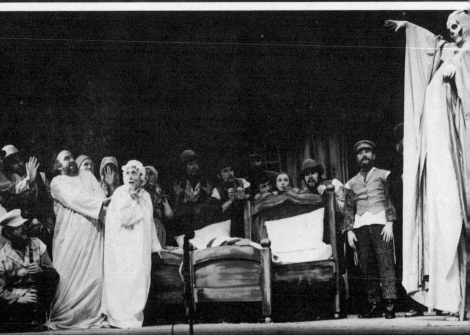

Both: Combi Press Service

Mounting the Amsterdam production was not the technical nightmare the Israeli experience had been, but it was far from trouble-free—mainly because the Carré was unprepared to handle *Fiddler*'s complexities. The technical director was determined to follow his usual procedure of employing a partly different stage crew every night, which meant that each performance would be technically sloppy and overall improvement would be almost impossible to achieve. However, he finally agreed to change his procedure to meet *Fiddler*'s demands.

One of the problems we had to deal with—and live with— long before the show was in performance was that the lady in charge of acquiring props was totally inept. Two factors kept her from being replaced: She had translated our play into Dutch and she was the wife of the producer.

Nepotism didn't end with the prop department. The associate producer informed me before I met the cast that we'd been fortunate in signing as Lazar Wolf one of the country's leading actors—his father. Unfortunately the man was well into his eighties, couldn't possibly do any of the dancing required in "To Life" and was unable to step on the moving turntable without falling and risking serious injury. On the second day of rehearsal, I had to replace him; he remained in the company as a bit player with a couple of lines to speak.

Although not cast because of any family ties, one of the singers who'd been chosen by our musical director stood a lofty six feet, eight inches. As the villagers made their single-file entrance at the top of "Tradition," it was impossible to watch anyone except our giant Anatevkan. He had an excellent baritone, so we retired him to the wings, where his needed voice was heard in all the big numbers. He also became an efficient assistant stage manager.

In at least two instances in Amsterdam, we were burdened by overconscientiousness, and here the Dutch more than lived up to their reputation for neatness. They were meticulous to a fault. The recording company was so eager to produce a flawless recording of *Anatevka* that a grueling two-and-a-half days were spent achieving what is normally done in one. The result was that the actors and musicians were so exhausted by the endless takes and retakes that what was finally produced, although letter-perfect, was the most lifeless album of *Fiddler* ever made.

The costumes created for *Anatevka* were similarly lifeless, bearing no relation to the lives of the characters who were supposed to wear them. The costumes were simply *too* good—too finely stitched, too crisp and new looking. The careful Dutch ladies who made them had wanted them neat, clean and nicely detailed. Fortunately, Pat Zipprodt was scheduled to be in Amsterdam in time for technical rehearsals, but it was a chore even for her to convince the costume people that the clothes had to look old and imperfectly made.

She explained, for example, that Motel's suit should not fit particularly well, that the trousers should be very obviously patched and worn. Motel, though a conscientious tailor, would be the last person to be concerned about his own clothes. Pat's constant awareness of character is, of course, one of the qualities that has made her a superior designer. The actors regarded her lovingly as a sorceress, for day by day—by adding a rip here, a patch there, a let-out seam for this one, a special aging or dye job for that one—she was bringing needed character to the costumes.

Paul Kijzer was rightly pleased with his decision to bring Pat to Amsterdam. The expense had been more than offset by good results. Two months after the Amsterdam opening, *Fiddler* was presented for the first time in England. Paul flew in for the London opening, and at intermission he came up to me. "Pat Zipprodt wasn't here, was she?" he asked. I shook my head. "That's what I thought," he said.

Pat had not been asked to supervise the construction of costumes for the London production, but the costume crew worked with her sketches. If the clothes fell short of the perfection that Pat's presence would have ensured, this was a minor quibble. The overall technical excellence in London was, at the very least, on a par with New York. Hal Prince and his London partner, Richard Pilbrow, were the producers, with Pilbrow doubling as the lighting designer. His work was even richer and more evocative than the lighting on the original New York production had been. After the chaotic Tel Aviv and Amsterdam rehearsals, which had provided fledgling stage managers with on-the-job training, it was good to work with a smoothly efficient stage managerial staff.

For Tommy and me to open the Amsterdam production on December 21, 1966, and then plunge into another production of the same show less than two weeks later would have been unthinkable—if the next production had been anywhere other than London. But the opportunity to live there awhile and do a show in the West End was much too tempting to pass up. And how welcome it was to know that we would be rehearsing the show in our own language.

But the rehearsal period proved tedious and difficult for both of us. After weeks of coaching, teaching, molding and prodding our Dutch company and crew into becoming a single, cohesive mass, the prospect of having to start all over again was very depressing. We did manage to muster enthusiasm for the job; it was essential if we were to excite the actors' imagination and interest sufficiently to lead them to do their best work. But after the London opening, Tom and I agreed that it was folly to do back-to-back productions of the same show; the effect was debilitating emotionally and physically. All I felt that February 16 was how happy I would be if I never had to look at a pair of Sabbath candlesticks, a prayer shawl or a yarmulke again.

Soon after rehearsals began, Richard Pilbrow confessed to me that he had misgivings about the show. "I know it's been a huge success everywhere," he said, "but I'm very much afraid that we might be coming up with the first flop. I just don't know if our West End audiences can be particularly stirred by the plight of Jewish peasants in Czarist Russia." There did seem to be little excitement in London about our forthcoming opening, certainly nothing to match the anticipation ignited by the announcement that Barbra Streisand would appear there in *Funny Girl* or that Mary Martin would do *Hello, Dolly!* There seemed to be more interest in Inga Swenson, who was rehearsing and hoping to re-create her New York success in *110 in the Shade*. Topol was, of course, a virtual unknown then, and the advance sale of *Fiddler* tickets was modest.

Richard was also concerned because Topol had an accent. The Israeli actor was being coached daily on his English, but his marked continental dialect would never disappear. Richard wondered if Topol's accent, in contrast to the precise English speech of the rest of the company, would be disconcerting. I wondered, too, for I had always agreed with Jerry Robbins's decision to have no actors with accents in the cast; he had felt that even one noticeable accent would destroy the illusion that the characters were all speaking their native tongue.

Topol had been cast because no major British actors were available who possessed Tevye's essential qualities. Alfie Bass, who played the part eventually, was approached, but he was committed to a television series, and both Peter Ustinov and Leo McKern felt the role should be played by a Jewish actor. Topol's presence in the cast was both a blessing and a danger. His rough, raw vitality helped the other actors as they groped to find the earthy peasant existence of their characters. But it was just possible that Topol would unwittingly expose the chasm that separated Sholom Aleichem's simple country folk from the natural polish of most British actors.

The actors' clipped accents continued to bother me, but I kept reminding myself that an Englishman seeing the Broadway production might be similarly disturbed to hear Russians and Jews speaking with what he might call an "American accent." However, there was a certain well-bred gentility in many of the British performers that put them closer to Kensington than to Kiev. Our no-nonsense constable, no matter how we dressed him, seemed straight out of Sandhurst. And the behavior of our impoverished Anatevkans often suggested Charles Dickens rather than Sholom Aleichem. It was Tommy's feeling that because England hadn't had a peasant class since medieval times, the characters' earthy qualities and the concept of a peasant community that was both proud and humble were entirely foreign to our actors. Perhaps he was right.

American theatre folk tend to have a built-in inferiority complex when comparing American and British actors. For one thing, the training and opportunities most young actors are exposed to in England are infinitely better. Much promising talent in the States gets lost for lack of theatres in which to learn and grow. For another, the native ability of many talented Americans was ruined in the fifties and early sixties when they fell victim to charlatan gurus preaching extreme pseudo-Method nonsense. London has a geographical advantage over New York, of course, for it is the center of film activities as well as the theatre. English films, over the years, have been so meticulously and perfectly cast, down to the smallest bit-player, that most Americans assume that an endless supply of first-rate talent resides in London. Unhappily, I discovered that the supply is by no means endless. Of the four foreign *Fiddler*s I have staged, the general level of the original London cast was undeniably the lowest.

Granted, there were some fine actors in the production— Miriam Karlin, Paul Whitsun-Jones, Sandor Elès, Linda Gardner and Anna Tzelniker—but it was disheartening to have to work with even a few barely adequate performers, and in London, of all places. The reason, though, might simply have been the lack of interest on the part of London's better actors in a musical like *Fiddler,* and pessimism about its chances for survival in the West End.

Aside from Topol, the only actor in the London company who was not British born was our Perchik, Sandor Elès. He had emigrated from Hungary after the 1956 revolution and thus had a grasp of Eastern European life that he unconsciously communicated to the other actors. The anglicization of Sandor had been complete; he had the barest trace of an accent, and he affected an upper-class priggishness that I doubt he brought with him from Hungary. But his lofty, lordly attitude added just the right note of arrogance to make his Perchik interesting.

I was warned before I met him that Sandor might be troublesome—for one thing, he was refusing to grow a beard. There were movie and TV offers he wanted to pursue; having a beard would have been inconvenient. I was not in a position to apply

A high point in the "Bottle Dance." London production.

Photograph by Zoe Dominic

strong pressure on him, because by the time I reached London, Sandor had a signed contract and had made it clear that he would wear a false beard in the production. So I attempted to finesse him, when I met him at a preproduction party at Richard Pilbrow's home. Most of the men were already sporting stubbled cheeks and chins, but Sandor was clean shaven.

We chatted pleasantly for a few minutes. Then, as I was about to leave him, I said, "It's really too bad about your beard problem, but I guess you have no choice, have you?" I walked away, and as I had hoped, he came after me to ask what was "too bad" about it. "Well," I began carefully, "you'll look terribly phony surrounded by all those real beards. I'm afraid it'll greatly affect the way the audience and the critics accept you in the role."

"I see," he said thoughtfully. A few days later, at the first reading of the show, he appeared with the scrubby beginnings of a nice dark beard.

Hal Prince arrived in London before previews, and immediately expressed disappointment with several of the performers—

two in particular whom I had wanted, but had been unable, to replace. His agitation was about to boil over into anger at *me* when I reminded him that he had never invited me to participate in the casting sessions that had taken place the preceding year. He looked at me a long moment. "You're right," he said. "I'll never do that to a director again." I had never liked Hal so well, nor respected him so much, as I did at that particular moment.

Eventually, we were joined in London by Joe Stein, Jerry Bock and conductor Milton Greene, on temporary leave from the New York production to give whatever assistance he could to Gareth Davies, our talented musical director at Her Majesty's Theatre. What was even more effective in spurring the company to maximum output and optimum attentiveness, in that preopening period, was the expected arrival of Jerome Robbins.

Although the spirit of Robbins hangs over every production of *Fiddler*, the London version was the only one outside New York to which he directed any personal attention. Everyone, from Topol on down, was anxious about the way Jerry would

react. Tommy and I were queried continually, but we offered
no clues and made no predictions as to what he might say. Truly
we didn't know. It was possible that he would look at the show,
say "It's fine," and spend the next several days going to other
plays in town. Or he might well say, "Cancel the opening. We're
going to rehearse two more weeks."

Jerry arrived in London the afternoon of the first public performance. A snowstorm had stranded him twelve hours at Kennedy Airport in New York, so he entered London looking
rumpled and weary. Tommy and I were as nervous as the actors,
for we knew that if he was in a black mood, nothing was going
to look good to him. There was much tension onstage when he
met the cast before the run-through. Needless to say, they
knocked themselves out for him. Their tension helped them;
they had never been so good before.

Tommy remembered the night, some time after *West Side
Story* had opened, when he and the other dancers looked off
into the wings and saw Jerry standing there—an unsmiling
figure all in black: black beard, black raincoat and black
sweater. Jerry was just watching, but as he stood there, the
performance level soared immeasurably. "Afterward we created the 'Best-Performance-After-Seeing-Jerry-Standing-in-the
Wings-Watching Award,'" says Tommy. But it would have
been hard to single out the most deserving recipient in London
that afternoon; everyone was very much affected by Jerry's
presence.

When the run-through was over, Jerry turned to Tommy and
me. "It's fine," he said, to our great relief. "It's all up there, but
there are a few things I'll want to play with in the next few
days." He jumped up on the stage to congratulate the actors;
they too were obviously relieved. He told them how pleased he
was with what they were doing and urged them to bear in mind
that the one element that had always been most important to
him in the show was *pride*. I watched him, his silvery beard
etched against the nubbly wool of his sweater, as he walked
through the opening moments of "Tradition," pointing out the

Photograph by Zoe Dominic

Tevye (Topol, left) and friends after hearing they must leave Anatevka.

basic qualities that should be present in the characters. With his head held high, he moved as he wanted all of them to move, projecting the pride and dignity they should feel in being Anatevkans, each time they set foot on the stage. The actors were enthralled; it was a perfect way to prepare them for their first audience that night.

Very little of consequence was actually done to the show in the days that followed. But Jerry worked like an industrious gem merchant, bringing individual moments to a brighter and richer luster. He made *little* changes, taking care of niggling problems that were never solved to his satisfaction in the original production; there were also things that with the passage of time he wanted to do differently now. He spent some time with a few of the minor actors who still needed attention. He also worked with Topol, whose performance, though toned down considerably, had been broad from the very beginning. Only one small trauma took place during this time, and it involved not Tevye but our Tzeitel, a lovely young actress named Rosemary Nicols, for whom *Fiddler* was her first important show.

Rosemary was not only talented but also blessed with a kind of natural beauty that couldn't help drawing attention to itself. Jerry liked her, but her attractiveness bothered him. She didn't look to him like a girl who would want anyone like Motel, a poor tailor. He watched her for a few days and finally said to me, "Put glasses on her." I knew what her reaction would be, and I wasn't happy to be the one who had to tell her. She tried to choke back tears at the first mention of glasses and said she would appeal directly to Jerry. I urged her not to, to simply play along with him and wear them. "Maybe in a few days he'll take them away," I suggested. "But if you make a scene now, he'll get annoyed and you'll end up with warts on your face." She played along and wore the glasses. She still managed to look appealing and attractive, but she was much more believable—and she knew it.

"A triumph," said the *Evening Standard,* after *Fiddler* opened. A "magnificent musical," said the *Sunday Citizen;* "Superb, that rare thing: a popular work of art," said the *Sunday Express;* and the *Daily Express* called it "a major musical in the masterly levels of *My Fair Lady* and Robbins' own *West Side Story.*" Despite our various concerns about accents, the receptivity of English audiences and the unevenness of the performances, the show was unanimously acclaimed in London.

The Paris production (*Un Violon sur le Toit*) opened more than two and a half years later, in November 1969, at the Théâtre Marigny. The man who played Tevye was good, though not among the best actors to have played the part. But the company, overall, gave the best-acted and best-sung performance of the show that I have ever seen.

My first shock, on arriving in France, was to be told by one of the show's four producers, Hubert de Malet, that we would rehearse afternoons and evenings until midnight. There I was, in Paris at last, and I was not to be allowed to enjoy the city's fabled restaurants and night life. I ad-libbed some nonsense about the importance of working only the morning and afternoon hours, because the actors would be portraying peasants who rose at dawn and such a schedule would be better "preparation" for them. M. de Malet's English was limited, and though he was confused by my argument, he agreed to it. The actors were appalled at the idea of working in the morning, but I dined extremely well during the next two months.

By the time I went to Paris I was hardened and no longer affected by dire predictions about the fate of the show. I was prepared for them and for other dangers as well. And since Tel Aviv, I had been wary of translations. Even so, some of the idiomatic expressions that had been inserted into the French script slipped by me. It was not until we were well into rehearsals that I realized that some of the lines were getting snickers from the company—because off-color material had been added. When I protested, the translator (one of the producers, as it happened) lectured me on the sophisticated nature of French audiences who, he said, expected such things from musicals.

The double entendres were not the only excesses the translator had indulged himself in. He had also gone overboard at times in his desire to wring tears out of the audience, upsetting the delicate balance between legitimate sentiment and blatant sentimentality. *Fiddler's* second act has more than its share of sentiment, but understatement had always been the best way to approach it. I insisted that my producers were truly underrating, if not insulting, their audiences, but they would not be swayed. As a last resort I threatened to report back to Robbins and Stein, and the offending material was finally removed.

The script problem was only a minor skirmish compared to the major battle over *Fiddler's* costumes. The producers were almost paranoid in their fear of what Parisian audiences would accept or reject as appropriate costuming. I didn't know until

Archives Lipnitski

*"Such a match for my Tzeitel!" Golde (Maria Murano) re-
acting to the plan proposed by Yente (Florence Blot). Paris.*

I arrived that they had received permission not to use Pat
Zipprodt's original designs. "Paris audiences will never accept
the dreary, depressing costumes you used in New York and
London," I was told.

Donald Cardwell, an American designer living in Paris, created the wardrobe for the production. He presented his sketches
to me just before rehearsals were under way. In the beginning,
the actors would all be dressed in various shades of yellow and
pale green (because it was spring then, I believe)—which
would change to blue tones in the wedding scene, because, according to Cardwell, we needed a visual progression from the
play's lighter moments to its darker ones. Tevye's daughters
were to wear delicate fabrics and cute puffed sleeves that exposed bare arms. The dream sequence was to be performed
entirely in the dark—with iridescent fabrics that suggested
nothing more to me than the Halloween show at Radio City
Music Hall.

I tried my best to be tactful, however. "The people in this show are poor peasants, and they must look that way," I said. "What's more, Tevye's daughters must be dressed for farm work and cow-milking. They don't wake up one morning and say, 'Oh, it's spring, time to put on our pretty yellows and greens.'" My choreographer, Irene Claire, was as appalled as I. (Tommy had not been free to come to Paris; Irene, who had assisted him in London, ably handled the choreography.)

The two of us met with the producers, and I told them I thought the self-conscious color scheme was a designer's conceit and had nothing to do with poverty-stricken people who were lucky to have anything to wear. I objected to the neatly tailored military uniform that had been designed for Perchik; the suit created for Motel, which looked like off-the-rack Cardin; the rabbi's super-elegant prayer shawl, which the chief rabbi of Moscow would have envied; and the fact that the fiddler, symbol of humble ghetto life, was to wear a top hat made of silk.

The answer I received was what I might have expected: "Richard, you must understand that Parisian audiences are like no others in the world. They're used to elegance and beauty; they would be disgusted and revolted by shabbiness."

I explained that I wasn't asking for shabby or depressing clothes. I had always felt that Pat's costumes were not only appropriate for the time, place and people but also wonderfully colorful, and in their own unobtrusive way, attractive. As to "elegance and beauty," *Fiddler* couldn't begin to compete with the whipped-cream-and-candy-cane look of popular operettas playing in Paris, nor should it ever attempt to. I felt certain the producers were underestimating the intelligence of Parisian theatregoers, and I told them that "if your audiences aren't going to accept the show as it was conceived—and *I* think they will —then you shouldn't really be doing it. And you certainly shouldn't be pretending to give them the American production they have heard about."

Cardwell might well have agreed with me, but he could say nothing, as he had been hired specifically to "pretty up" the production. The producers themselves made the final decisions,

A shock to the wedding guests—Perchik taking Hodel's hand to dance. Gérard Paquis and Janet Clair: in France.

Archives Lipnitski

and wanting to keep both Irene and me hard at work, they reluctantly gave in. Slowly, piece by piece, changes were made, and if the costumes were never totally right, they were close enough to what had been intended so as not to violate the show's integrity. Inexplicably, the designer missed two splendid opportunities to create costumes where faded elegance and beauty would have been appropriate. But Tzeitel's wedding dress and the gown worn by the ghost of Fruma-Sarah were plain and drab compared to what Pat had created.

Joe Stein arrived in Paris in time for the opening. He was as pleased as I to see that despite the producers' fears and anxieties, *Fiddler* was given a magnificent reception. Several critics pointed out that *Fiddler* might well break the jinx for American musicals, which had traditionally failed in Paris. It was reassuring to note that Parisians reacted exactly as audiences elsewhere had. They had been neither put off nor shocked by the actors' appearing in clothes that peasants could conceivably have worn, nor had the critics. The press' attitude was summed up by these

words in *Le Monde*: "The French barriers against Anglo-American musical comedy were broken down with this show . . ."

Perhaps *Fiddler on the Roof* makes special demands of its audiences. Perhaps its broad themes involve people so deeply that their cultural identification and their own private prejudices are subordinated. To date *Fiddler* has been seen not only in England, France, Holland and Israel, but also, as has been noted, in South Africa, Austria and both East and West Germany. In addition, there have been productions in Mexico, Argentina, Brazil, Czechoslovakia, Yugoslavia, Australia, New Zealand, Turkey, Spain, Greece, Japan, Norway, Sweden, Denmark, Iceland, Rhodesia, Switzerland—and, incredible for its small size, Finland has had fifteen different productions.

No doubt each time a production was about to be mounted, in each of these far-flung countries, there have been those within the company who felt that in that particular place and at that particular time, *Fiddler* simply would not work. But the show has never missed. Its universality has always enabled

The wedding scene as it was staged in East Berlin.

Arwid Lagenpusch

154

"Some are driven away by edicts, others by silence." Fyedka (Johannes Felsenstein) confronting Tevye (Rudolf Asmus) in final scene. East Berlin Fiddler.

Arwid Lagenpusch

Tevye (Hisaya Morishige, at right), Lazar Wolf and fellow Anatevkans drinking and celebrating the good news in "To Life." Toyko production.

people of many faiths and widely differing cultures to identify with it. The critic for Japan's *Tokyo Shimbun* declared that "the musical is interesting as a kind of bitter-sweet comedy even to those who are quite ignorant of the particular Jewish customs and manners, faith and philosophy." And in the *Sankei Shimbun*, *Fiddler* was described as "a musical which speaks of the truth of life. A classic."

When Joe Stein attended *Fiddler*'s Tokyo opening, a young man approached him during intermission and asked if he were connected with the show. Joe said that he was. The young man asked if it were true that *Fiddler* had been a big hit in America. "Yes, it's true," Joe assured him. "What's the matter—don't you like it?" The young man looked puzzled. "Of course I like it," he insisted, "but it's so Japanese."

Top: *The kitchen, Yente visiting Golde as Motel arrives to see Tzeitel.*

Bottom: *Tevye* (left), *rabbi and villagers preparing to leave Anatevka.*

All: courtesy of Jacobson & Harmon

11

Bomba & Lex
& Topol & Ivan

STARTING WITH Zero, the role of Tevye has often been played
by men who were difficult to work with. The role requires an
actor of enormous ego and unshakable assurance, or else
Tevye's presence will not be dominant, as it surely must be. For
most of the Tevyes, the more successful they become, the more
difficult they become.

The four Tevyes I have directed were entirely different—a
remarkable contrast if I were to appraise them collectively. The
first one swung from no-confidence to overconfidence. The second was perfect in every way and, incredibly, without being
temperamental in the bargain. The third, though he was erratic
and his judgment was often faulty, had authority and style, and
he towered over a company that was rarely up to his level; the
result was impressive enough for him to win the role in the
screen *Fiddler*. The last one was primarily an opera singer who

Mula & Haramaty
Bomba J. Zur, Tevye in the Tel Aviv production.

disliked rehearsing and was happier just copying other Tevyes rather than trying to make the part his own.

Until *Fiddler* came along, Bomba J. Zur had not been considered a serious actor by his fellow Israelis. Although he had been roundly applauded for playing Eliza Doolittle's father, he had not been required to carry *My Fair Lady* all by himself. Nothing in Bomba's experience to date had prepared him to tackle a part as many faceted as Tevye. But in his first readings Bomba conveyed a great deal of the humor, warmth and musical comedy zest we were seeking. After hearing him, I felt certain that he could play the sober and more dramatic second act if he simply trusted himself, his instincts and me.

But at first he trusted neither of us. He was so afraid of not being accepted in the serious scenes that he refused to let himself go with the comedy. His greatest concern throughout rehearsals was, "It's not too funny, is it?"—as if by provoking laughter he would make it impossible for the audience to believe him in somber moments. *Fiddler's* first act is generally light and amusing, and the darker second act works best if its mood contrasts with that of the first. Again and again I assured him that Act One must be funny—and reminded him that one of the principal reasons for his having been cast was that he was a talented comedian.

That he was frightened at first was to be expected. Unfortunately, this fear paralyzed him. Instead of getting better day by day, he was getting slightly worse, more and more tentative in his playing of the drama and consistently flattening out the comedy. The monologues, in which Tevye talks to himself or communicates his inner thoughts to God, were especially forbidding because of the rapid shifts in emotion that were called for. The monologues were also hard to sing; though not so melodic as a song might be, they demanded strict attention to phrasing and inflection. Bomba preferred speaking them; it took a great deal of persuading to get him to actually sing them.

Bomba worked extremely hard trying to conquer the role and his own insecurity in it. He worked hardest and was most responsive when he and I rehearsed alone, away from other members of the company. I once spent an entire day with him, and he was excellent; remarkable progress was made then. But as soon as he was back onstage with the rest of the cast, his fears returned and he froze. And as we came nearer and nearer to facing our first audience, his anxiety quotient soared.

Two days before previews began, he was distant and quite obviously depressed, wanting to be left alone and not eager to hear or accept the notes I had for him. For the first time angry words flared between us. But I couldn't let him alone; he just wasn't good enough. I took him to dinner and urged him as emphatically as I could not to be nervous about being nervous—it was, I insisted, a common and perfectly normal feeling. Frankly,

I'd be upset if an actor playing Tevye wasn't a little nervous before the first performances.

At the final run-through he did relax somewhat, and much of the warmth of which he was capable finally came through. The first audience threw him, as expected, and his performance was generally subdued. His timing was off, and he missed many of the laughs he should have been getting. But the barrier had finally been broken; he knew he wasn't going to be laughed or hooted out of the theatre. His work improved with each succeeding audience.

Then less than a week before the opening, I was stunned to see him begin to walk through his scenes. All the vitality and energy his tension had provided was now disappearing. Complacency was taking hold, and his performance was crumbling, bringing the entire show down with it. Where I had once strained to relieve his anxiety, I now had to scare him to death —to predict artistic disaster for him—in order to jar him out of his complacency and reestablish some of the tautness the part called for. By opening night a much-sought happy medium was reached and Bomba was fine.

I was never able to return to Israel, but I know Bomba had a hard time sustaining the role throughout the run. The part exhausted him so much that Shmuel Rudensky was brought in to play a few performances every week. And for a brief period Chaim Topol played some of the matinees. Although he has never admitted it to me, perhaps Topol had London on his mind even then.

From Topol I inadvertently discovered that Bomba had changed a number of things in the show after I was safely out of the country. As we began work on Tevye's monologues at our London rehearsals, Topol started to talk them instead of sing them. I urged him to do them the way he had done them in Tel Aviv, and to my surprise he said he had done them just that way.

"You mean you didn't play the show the way Bomba did?" I asked. "I certainly did," he replied. "That's what Bomba was doing when *I* saw the show." I had no answer for that one. No doubt Bomba had made other "improvements" as well, but I wasn't at all eager to find out about them.

I had no such worries about Lex Goudsmit, our Tevye in Amsterdam. Like Bomba, Lex was not an important actor in his country at the time he was cast, but he'd had years of training in repertory companies, playing everything from Shakespeare to Chayevsky. He had performed with "pop" musical groups and had sung opera. He was a reliable actor whom *Fiddler* turned into a star.

From the very first rehearsal it was obvious that Lex and I were on the same wavelength. He had an intuitive feeling about the show and about the way Tevye should be played. He was responsive and enthusiastic. Whenever I described a particular piece of stage business for him, I could see his eyes light up and he would begin to chuckle. He knew just what he was going to do, and he relished the prospect of doing it. He wasn't afraid of the comedy, nor did he go overboard trying to be funny. Lex had every quality Tevye required: warmth, depth, humor, presence, confidence and a fine baritone voice. Even his physical look was perfect—what more could I ask for? The fact that he spoke English well was another plus; there was no communication gap between us. I was delighted when Richard Pilbrow decided to import him as a replacement in the London *Fiddler* three years later.

When Lex finished touring *Fiddler* in Holland, his next assignment was to play Sancho Panza in *Man of La Mancha,* which I returned to Amsterdam to direct. It was a fine performance—I should say a heroic one, although his specific display of heroism occurred backstage and was unseen by the audience. It took place on the most horrendous opening night I've ever lived through or heard about.

Our Don Quixote was a brilliant classical actor named Guus Hermus, whom I called "Gus," as the actual Dutch pronunciation of his name was impossible for an American to effect. Hermus is to Dutch audiences what Laurence Olivier is to the English-speaking theatre. His versatility is remarkable; about the only thing he had never done onstage before was sing in a musical.

Lex Goudsmit, who played Tevye first in Holland and later in England.

Guus was a compelling figure in *La Mancha:* tall, lean and as gaunt as the hollow-cheeked Quixote was expected to be. Although he lacked a trained singing voice, he did quite well by the songs. But he was highly sensitive and insecure about his singing. He was also fiercely temperamental.

At one of our final rehearsals, a minor technical mishap occurred right after the show began. Guus left the stage shouting and screaming, completely distraught because something had gone wrong. He was so angry he couldn't be reasoned with, so there was nothing we could do but cancel that evening's work. Our technical problems were ultimately solved, but these were not our vital concern. Knowing how uncertain Guus continued to be, we nurtured the nightmare of his becoming upset with one thing or another and walking off the stage in front of an audience, although it was difficult to believe that anyone would be capable of doing that.

Man of La Mancha opened at the Theatre Carré on December 21, 1968, two years to the day after *Fiddler* had opened at the same theatre. I was seated next to my American choreographer, Lola Braxton, who was as nervous as I because of Guus.

The show got off to a good start, but in his first number Guus made a couple of mistakes. They were minor vocal bloopers, not at all serious, but Guus seemed unstrung by them. He became more tense with each passing minute. By the time he launched into "The Impossible Dream," Lola and I were clutching each other, holding on dearly, praying that he would get through it all right and hardly daring to look at the stage. Then the unthinkable happened.

On one of the high notes, near the climax of the song, his voice cracked, and Guus stopped singing. A flash of anger crossed his face, and he threw down his lance and shield and stalked off the stage. The orchestra stopped playing; there was total silence in the theatre. While sitting there, frozen with disbelief, staring at the empty stage, I thought, "Well, there it goes—months of work and thousands of guilders."

But Lex Goudsmit was waiting in the wings to make his next entrance. As Guus stormed offstage, Lex grabbed him. "You *have* to go back," Lex said. "No matter what has gone wrong, you *must* go back. You have a responsibility to the audience, to the company and to me—and *you are going back*." He spun Guus around and literally pushed him out on the stage. Guus picked up his shield and lance, and glanced into the orchestra pit; the conductor resumed "The Impossible Dream." This time Guus sang it perfectly. The rest of the performance came off flawlessly, and Guus received an ovation at the end, although the press did take him to task in subsequent days for his unprofessional behavior.

The Tevye I worked with after Lex Goudsmit was Chaim Topol, the actor who ultimately won the role in the film version. He was also the youngest Tevye I ever directed.

Topol was the last person to be cast in the London production. With the rest of the company already set and no Tevye in sight, producer Richard Pilbrow had even tried to bring

Herschel Bernardi over from New York, but arrangements couldn't be worked out. Then Richard received a letter from Annette Meyers, Hal Prince's secretary, suggesting that he look at Topol, who was appearing in the movie *Sallah*. Annette wrote that the Israeli actor had been only twenty-nine when the film was made, but in it he played a sixty-two-year-old. The Pilbrows, Richard and his wife Viki, saw the film and arranged to bring Topol to London at their expense. It was a gamble, but the signs were good: His name in Hebrew, Chaim (meaning "life") Topol ("tree") had an earthy ring to it.

Joe Stein and Jerry Bock were in London to help cast the production, and they were as surprised as the Pilbrows when Topol stepped onto the stage of the Drury Lane Theatre—a young-looking man whose broken English had a peculiar Franco-American accent. But then he read two scenes and sang "If I Were a Rich Man," and according to Joe, "he was just marvelous. I thought, 'If he's this good now, imagine how great he'll be when he starts rehearsing.' We didn't know yet that he had played the part before, in Hebrew. But it didn't matter. We'd still have been enormously impressed."

It was a unanimous decision, and Richard went up on the stage to say, "Mr. Topol, we'd love to have you play the role for us in London." The actor looked shocked. "You mean—" he started, choosing his words carefully, "you really want—*me*—to play Tevye—in London?" And Richard replied, "Yes, we do." Topol stared at him and finally said, "May I take your word as an English gentleman?" Richard extended his hand to Topol, and they shook hands on it.

Whenever the name Chaim Topol was mentioned in the days that followed, none of the Pilbrows' friends or associates could pronounce it, so at the time the actor received his one-year contract he lost half his name. It was decided that only his last name be used—that it would be easier for the public to grasp and also be more impressive. The stark singularity of "Topol" suggested that if one had never heard of the actor, one certainly *should* have.

My first private meeting with Topol took place in a delicatessen in Soho. I was struck by his exuberance and by his charm—

Photograph by Zoe Dominic
Topol, the original London Tevye—later to repeat his role in the film.

and by the fact that his thickly matted hair and dark beard (already full grown by then) gave him an Eastern European appearance—which was not surprising, since his mother was Polish and his father was Russian. He seemed ageless and at the same time any age, neither very young nor very old. There was an intensity to his nature that was riveting, and I knew that audiences would feel it too. As we walked down Shaftesbury Avenue together, he was completely ignored, even with his full beard. But two months later he was to be the toast of London, a much-pampered and sought-after celebrity.

Because Topol had done *Fiddler* before, my life was somewhat easier during the early stages of rehearsal. I could devote my energy and attention to the other actors. Topol remembered most of his blocking from Tel Aviv and could be left alone much of the time, until the other principals were firmly on their feet. Once in a while, though, he surprised me.

The first act of *Fiddler* ends with the pogrom that shatters the gaiety of Tzeitel and Motel's wedding, as the Russian constable and his men overturn tables, smash dishes and hurl wedding gifts to the ground. Afterward, as the celebrants sadly pick through the debris, Tevye crosses downstage, looks up helplessly to God and makes a shrugging gesture that seems to ask, "Why?" as the curtain falls.

When we reached the end of Act One in our blocking rehearsal, Topol crossed down center, looked up to God—and then his fist suddenly shot straight up in a vehemently defiant gesture. "What's that?" I managed to ask from my seat in the first row. "That's the way I end Act One," he answered. "No," I said, "that is *not* the way you end Act One." He insisted that it was, and I said we would discuss it at lunch.

Later, at the restaurant, I asked him about the gesture. "I must play it that way," he explained, "because I'm tired of the 'poor Jew' who's always bowing and scraping to God. That's the European World War II Jew, and I'm a Sabra. I've got more guts than that." I assured him that though his feelings as a Sabra were well and good, they had nothing to do with Tevye or with *Fiddler*. There were no Sabras in 1905, nor was there an Israel, as we know it, then. There was no justification for him to impose his views on what Jews should or should not be. Tevye, I reminded him, was a simple, God-fearing man of his time.

Topol couldn't argue these points, and to his credit he didn't attempt to. He never made his power-to-the-people gesture again, although his Israeli nationalism remained as strong as ever. In June 1967, when the Six-Day War began, he tried to rush to his homeland immediately, but he couldn't get on a flight until the day before the shooting stopped. Even so, he was hailed as a hero when he returned to England, and his recording of "If I Were a Rich Man" soon climbed to Number Five on English "pop" music charts.

Like Zero Mostel, Topol had a natural flair for Tevye. He said the part gave him "an opportunity to put a tombstone on the grave of my grandfather." It was always startling in rehearsal to see his youthful body droop and adopt the motions and profile of a much older man. But also like Zero, he tended to overdo the comedy, to become too broad, to embellish to the point of excess. My main difficulty was in keeping him from getting so carried away with his low-comedy instincts that he would distort the characterization. Joe Stein and Jerry Bock were later helpful in convincing Topol that he was most effective when his work was simplest and most honest. And when Jerry Robbins arrived on the scene, he cautioned Topol about the dangers of excess.

By the time *Fiddler* opened, Topol was excellent. He had overcome most of his language problems. His performance had strength, conviction and great gusto, and it projected an oddly sensual nature that no other Tevye ever had. Jerry Bock and Joe rank his performance second to Zero's, but Sheldon, who flew to London soon after the opening, said, "Topol was the *best* Tevye. When he walked out onstage with that lumberjack's body and he grinned—with that gap in his teeth—my wife and I melted. It was like, 'Take us, we're yours.'"

And the critics were equally ecstatic. "Topol trudged triumphantly into our hearts," said the *Evening Standard*. "Once in a generation there suddenly arrives in our theatre a great star," proclaimed the *Evening News*. The *Sunday Citizen* called Topol's work "the performance of a lifetime," and *News of the World* said, "A bearded man in patched pants becomes king of London's musical stage, a star overnight."

Topol created a sensation in London theatre circles, and he quickly became identified with Tevye, just as Zero had in New York. In time he also identified the fortunes of the show with the quality of his performance. When Richard Pilbrow wanted him to extend his contract, he readily agreed—on the condition that the show would be closed when he finally left it. When Richard asked why, the actor explained that it was now his part and that nobody else in England could play it.

Pilbrow refused to make such a guarantee, and Topol left the show after a year—to be replaced first by Alfie Bass, later by Lex Goudsmit, and then Barry Martin. Four and a half years after it opened in London, *Fiddler* was still running there—and a second company had merrily toured the English provinces.

Just as Zero's performance had given *Fiddler* a leg-up on its rise to legendary success in the United States, Topol had certainly given the show a magnificent launching in England. But having worked in Amsterdam just prior to coming to London, Tom Abbott and I were so spoiled by Lex's work that I don't think we fully appreciated Topol's enormous talent.

Ivan Rebroff had already been signed for Tevye by the time I reached Paris in the fall of 1969, another instance of an actor's winning the role somewhat by default. Peter Ustinov (whose French is superb), Charles Aznavour and the French comedian Bourvil had been sought at some point, but none had

Ivan Rebroff, the Russian-German opera star who played Tevye in Paris.
Archives Lipnitski

wanted to do the part. Rebroff, an opera singer who had recently enjoyed great success on French TV, seemed a logical choice.

Ivan was a robust man with a big, booming voice and a commanding presence on the stage. He was of Russian-German extraction, and as his English was good, we had no trouble communicating. But, unfortunately, his French was terrible. He spent the months prior to rehearsals being tutored intensively, and he learned his part pretty much by rote. As I had taken only a six-week crash course in French before leaving New York, I was hardly the one to judge his competence, except by checking with our platoon of producers. One of them said that even *my* French was better than Ivan's, which was not encouraging news.

Ivan, unlike some Tevyes, was terribly cooperative—much *too* cooperative, in fact. He would do anything I told him, and he wanted me to tell him everything: what Zero had done at this point, what Topol had done in that scene. He wanted it all handed to him, every movement, every pause and gesture, every "take," every rise and fall of speech. An actor playing Tevye (or any part, for that matter) should bring as much of himself to the role as he can, projecting his own personality, offering his own interpretation, letting his own life experiences help shape his characterization. Ivan was loath to draw upon himself. He didn't trust his acting ability very much, preferring to lean more heavily on his singing talents, which were considerable—sometimes too considerable. His huge voice frequently had to be restrained.

It is often hard for trained singers to rein in some of their powers, to understate the musical qualities of a song they have to sing. Jerry Robbins cautioned Julia Migenes many times to keep "Far From the Home I Love" from becoming an aria. When Ivan unleashed his operatic flourishes on "If I Were a Rich Man," the effect was like beating a paper dragon with a sledgehammer. "Ivan, this is not *Boris Godunov*," I had to remind him. I also had to persuade him not to use his trick falsetto, which was every bit as famous in France as Zero's crossed eyes were in America, but its effect was not right for Tevye.

I soon learned that though opera singers like Ivan enjoy singing out sometimes, there are times when they don't enjoy singing at all, and rehearsing is not among their favorite pastimes.
Ivan was especially lazy about rehearsing; when the thought of
it displeased him, he would complain of a painful shoulder or
of symptoms of a head cold—any excuse he could manage. Or
he would fly off to Germany for a long weekend. When he did
rehearse, he wanted to sing in half voice, and at run-throughs
he would try to walk through the show—"marking it," merely
going through the motions and saying the words.

I had to remind him over and over that because he was playing Tevye he would be setting the pace for everyone. "If *you*
walk through the show, everyone else will walk through it," I
explained. "And I can't very well insist that the others work at
full pitch and sing at full voice if you're only whispering." He
would look at me like an injured puppy in need of affection, but
then continue marking it.

"Look," I said finally, "I must see you doing your best work;
otherwise I can't help you. How will I know if what you're
doing is right?" That seemed to register, and he began to give
more and function better. When the show opened, Ivan's performance was enthusiastically cheered, and the press showered
him with accolades. Said *France-Soir*: "There is only one adjec-
tive for him: fabulous. He fills the whole stage with his presence. Everyone knows his beautiful singing voice, but he is also
a delicious actor, possessing density, malice, humor and an ad-
mirable humanity." *Fiddler* finally drew out the best that was in
him without exposing what wasn't there.

The night after the opening I dropped by the Marigny in the
middle of Act One, just to see how things were going. As I
watched Tevye's scene with Tzeitel and Motel—when the young
people convince him to let them marry—I was stunned to hear
an off-color French expression that I'd had Ivan delete weeks
before, during rehearsals. At the intermission I went to his dressing room. He looked up from his dressing table, obviously surprised to see me. I said nothing, but he knew what I was thinking. "Oh, my goodness," he burbled, "I thought you'd left for
Italy." Indeed I did fly to Italy the next day, but that experience

taught me to stay close to a production for at least a few days after it opens.

Joe Stein was the only one of *Fiddler's* creators who was in Paris for the opening. Walking with me to our beautiful theatre in the Champs-Elysées gardens before the final preview, he told me how pleased he was with the production, which he had watched take final shape. But he was even more excited about the fact that Topol had been cast in the screen *Fiddler*. I said nothing. Reading my thoughts, he said, "You like Lex Goudsmit a lot better, don't you?" I said that I did. Each of the Tevyes I'd worked with had been distinctive; each had had his virtues and flaws, strengths and weaknesses. There was no doubt that Topol was excellent, but Lex would always be my favorite.

Hayes Gordon, right, *Australia.*

Paul Rossi, below, *Buenos Aires.*

Both: courtesy of Jacobson & Harmon

Fotografoval D. Jar. Svoboda

Ladislav Pesek, Tevye in the Czechoslovakian production.

Yossi Yadin, the Israeli actor who portrayed Tevye in Vienna.
Foto Palffy

Eik Koch, left, *Denmark.*

Rudolf Asmus, below, *of East German production.*

Arwid Lagenpusch

Courtesy of Jacobson & Harmon

Uljas Kandolin as Tevye, with Eila Rinne as Golde in Helsinki Fiddler.

Cuneyt Gokcer, who played Tevye first in Turkey and later in Greece.

Courtesy of Jacobson & Harmon
Hisaya Morishige, the first Oriental Tevye, in Tokyo production.

Manolo Fabregas, Mexico.

Foto Felipe Morales

Lasse Kolstad, Oslo Tevye.

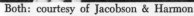

Both: courtesy of Jacobson & Harmon

Shimon Israeli, star of South African production.

Ljosmyndastofa Oli Pall Kristjansson

Robert Arnfinnsson, Tevye in the Reykjavik production, Iceland.

Antonio Garisa of Madrid, in the first Spanish-language version.

Courtesy of Jacobson & Harmon

Lennart Jansson

Bertil Norstrom (above), *the Swedish Tevye.*

Shmuel Rudensky (left) *of West Germany and Israel.*

Ilija Dzuvalekovsky (right) *of the Yugoslavian* Fiddler.

Both: courtesy of Jacobson & Harmon

12

To Lekenik,
Mala Gorica
and Martinska Ves

NORMAN JEWISON first saw *Fiddler on the Roof* at the Wednesday matinee following its New York opening. The performance was sold out, but through the William Morris agency, it was arranged for him to sit on a cushion in an aisle up in the balcony. Despite the less-than-comfortable circumstances, he was enormously moved by what he saw, and he felt that Jerome Robbins had given the show "a touch of genius." Jewison was not yet a major film director, and it never occurred to him that day that he would ever have a chance to direct the inevitable motion picture version of *Fiddler*.

Some weeks later Walter Mirisch was in New York with his wife to attend a Motion Picture Pioneers banquet. The Mirisch Production Company was the largest independent film company associated with United Artists. It was also the company that had purchased the screen rights to *West Side Story* and had produced that Academy Award-winning film for United Artists.

Joe Stein saw to it that the Mirisches had tickets for *Fiddler,* and the producer was captivated by it. "It was the most powerful show I'd ever seen on the stage," he says, "and I felt that I had to do it on the screen. I tried to convince United Artists to buy it right then, but though they liked it, they thought it was terribly ethnic. I was patient, though. Even though there was no film I'd ever wanted to do as much as *Fiddler,* I was willing to wait."

Mirisch knew that it could be mutually advantageous for both buyer and seller to wait. Big stage successes are often purchased for the screen long after they have opened because, from the film producer's point of view, to buy a property, shoot it, and then not be able to release it until the New York run has ended (which most Broadway producers insist on) can be very costly. Also, the creators of a show are often just as happy not to make a deal until their work has made a lot of money and earned even more prestige—which means their asking price can be higher. In *Fiddler's* case, that asking price had risen to $2.5 million by the time a deal with United Artists was finally made.

When *Fiddler* opened on Broadway in 1964, Norman Jewison's film credits consisted of only two Doris Day movies and a minor Tony Curtis comedy. Subsequently he was vaulted into the inner circle of established directors with *The Russians Are Coming, The Russians Are Coming* and *In the Heat of the Night,* which won the Oscar as the best picture of 1967. Chance put him squarely in line to direct *Fiddler.* People in Sholom Aleichem's world would have said it was *beshert*—deemed by fate—but more simply, Norman was suddenly a hot property. Also, he was in the right place with the right people at the right time.

He was in Boston filming *The Thomas Crown Affair* and had dinner one night at Locke-Ober's with Walter Mirisch and United Artists president David Picker. During the meal several projects were discussed, among them *Fiddler.* Jewison left the others early, as he had to be up at dawn for the next day's shooting. Mirisch and Picker decided to walk off their dinner, and within the next hour or so, Mirisch had convinced the UA president that Jewison was the man to handle *Fiddler.*

Jewison was delighted, of course, when he was asked to do the film, but he has always assumed that he was the second choice, after Jerome Robbins. Walter Mirisch says no: "I am aware of the immense contribution Jerry Robbins made to *Fiddler* on the stage, but would he have had any more to contribute to it as a film? I never went to him and would not have expected him to move toward me. I feel that Robbins is one of the most brilliant men I've ever dealt with in films, but on *West Side Story* he didn't seem able to pick up the tempo and style of picture-making. Things were just not getting done, and ultimately I had to split with him."

Jerry's experience with *West Side Story* in Hollywood was a personal disaster for him. It was one time when his usual long delay in signing contracts backfired, for even after he'd been shooting the film for many weeks, his contract was still being negotiated. This meant that he could still leave the project at any time, if he wished; it also meant that he could be fired— which he was, and co-director Robert Wise took over the film entirely. Robbins's assistants (Tom Abbott among them) oversaw musical numbers that had not yet been filmed.

From the beginning there had never been any doubt in Jewison's mind that he wanted *Fiddler* to have as much of the Robbins choreography as could be transferred to the screen. So Tommy was the logical person to adapt the original choreography and create new movement for sequences like the dream, which would be totally altered. In addition to the three productions Tom had worked on with me, he had also choreographed the first national company with Luther Adler, the West German company, and had both directed and choreographed the Oslo production.

I met Norman Jewison in Los Angeles in the summer of 1969, shortly before I left to stage the Paris *Fiddler*, and he asked me to help cast the movie from New York, because he knew that I was much more familiar with Broadway and Off-Broadway actors than either he or his Hollywood-based casting director, Lynn Stalmaster. I began my preliminary screening of actors at UA's New York offices in January 1970, working closely with

Stalmaster, who was seeing actors on the West Coast. By that time Topol had already been signed to play Tevye.

"I had known Topol from the film we made in Israel, *Cast a Giant Shadow*," says Mirisch. "In it he played a sixty-five-year-old Arab chief. I later met him in New York when he arrived for the release of *Sallah*, and I thought him the most extraordinary performer I'd ever seen. I didn't think of him for *Fiddler* until I read that he was to play Tevye in London, and then I thought what a good idea that was. Norman's and my first inclination had been to go with Zero Mostel, for Mostel had set the style for all the Tevyes. Then we decided that in his movie appearances Mostel tended to become 'too big.' We felt that Topol was potentially a better *movie* actor than Mostel. We also thought

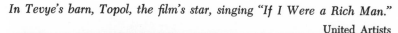

In Tevye's barn, Topol, the film's star, singing "If I Were a Rich Man."
United Artists

Topol was warmer and that his Tevye would have fire as well as the passion of relative youth."

According to Mirisch, Mostel was the only actor other than Topol who was actually considered, but a great many more, either directly or indirectly, made known their interest in playing Tevye, among them Danny Kaye, Walter Matthau, Herschel Bernardi, Rod Steiger, Danny Thomas, Richard Burton and even Frank Sinatra. I myself received several phone calls in New York from Robert Merrill's manager, who tried to convince me that Topol had decided not to do the film, but this was just an agent's wishful thinking.

Mirisch recalls: "When I read a squib in a trade paper that Topol was in his last two weeks of his London engagement, early in 1968, it galvanized me into action. I met Norman and his wife that night at the *Dr. Dolittle* premiere, and the moment I saw him I said, 'You and I are going to London to see Topol.'" The next day they were on a plane, and the following night they saw *Fiddler* at Her Majesty's Theatre.

"Topol lived up to everything I'd expected of him," says Norman. After the show he and Mirisch went backstage to congratulate Topol on his performance—it was Norman's first meeting with the actor. Later, as they walked back to the Dorchester Hotel, Jewison and Mirisch decided that Topol was their man. They returned to Los Angeles the next day and started negotiations.

Some time later Topol was disconcerted to learn that Norman wasn't Jewish, but eventually this proved no barrier between them. Although not born to the tradition, Norman learned it well. He understood the Tevye that Topol had created, and he knew how he wanted the character to come across on the screen. "I tried for that humble peasant quality in Topol's Tevye," he told me, "and at moments he does present the childlike quality of a man who isn't bright. But one reason I liked Topol's performance so much on the stage was that he projected his sense of destiny as, and pride in being, a Jew. His Tevye never loses dignity and strength; he is a man who knows who he is and where he's going."

For the screen, as it had been for the stage, the role of Golde was difficult to cast. "Norman and I both wanted Anne Bancroft," says Mirisch, "though I had little confidence that we'd get her." In addition to her proven talent, Norman especially liked her lean, bony look—an appeal that Maria Karnilova had exuded so effectively from her first auditions for the original production. Miss Bancroft wasn't interested in the part; she felt that *Fiddler* would be the man's picture. Norman reminded her that *The Graduate* hadn't been Mrs. Robinson's movie and that it hadn't hurt her reputation, but she remained adamant. So a widespread search was on.

Norman immediately vetoed many early suggestions, including Elaine May, Geraldine Page, Anne Jackson, Claire Bloom, Kim Stanley and Betty Garrett. But among those given some consideration were Colleen Dewhurst, Zoe Caldwell, Dorothy Loudon, Marian Seldes and opera star Beverly Sills. Maureen Stapleton was approached, but when she called and canceled her appointment with Norman for the third time, he blew up: "She won't even come to see me! What is this—a B movie?"

The top contenders for Golde were in California: Lee Grant and Norma Crane. Lee Grant had been Anne Bancroft's standby in *Two for the Seesaw* on Broadway (eventually replacing her in it) and was highly regarded as a talent on the stage as well as in movies and television. "She'd done *In the Heat of the Night* and *The Landlord* for Norman and me," says Walter Mirisch, "and she's a fine actress. But we had reservations about her physically. She has those finely chiseled features, and we doubted that she could ever look like a farm or peasant type. We considered Lee—and others—but we always came back to Norma Crane. She had the right physical quality."

When I learned that Miss Crane had been cast, I was struck by the ironic coincidence involving William Hanley's play, *Mrs. Dally Has a Lover,* which had made my association with *Fiddler* possible. Back in 1962 the actress that Hanley, producer Richard Barr and I had originally cast as Mrs. Dally was Norma Crane. But at a prerehearsal meeting with the playwright and me, she informed Bill that he would have to cut the

Yente: "It's about Lazar Wolf, the butcher!" Norma Crane, Molly Picon.

offstage sound effect of a toilet being flushed. Bill asked why. "Because I will not appear in a play that has a sound effect like that," she said.

Bill was barely able to keep from exploding. As calmly as possible, he told her that he had no intention of removing that sound effect. She held her ground and that was that. The next day we were back to auditioning Mrs. Dallys, and just three days before rehearsals were to begin, an actress we'd never heard of came to read: Estelle Parsons. She was cast, and at the end of that season she won the Theatre World Award for her performance.

Norma Crane (née Zuckerman) had once acted in a TV production of works by Sholom Aleichem (adapted by Morton Wishengrad), in which she played several Jewish mothers to the Jewish fathers portrayed by George Segal. She had replaced Kim Stanley in *Bus Stop* on Broadway and played the local tramp in the film version of *Tea and Sympathy*, but her career never really clicked. It was in the Mirisch Company's *They Call Me Mister Tibbs!* that she came to the attention of the Mirisches and Norman Jewison.

"After testing her," Norman says, "I felt that there was something deep, deep inside her. She had the right look to complement Topol. In films the visual look of the actor is very important. If he isn't right physically, he has an uphill battle. Some actors who work well in films would not necessarily seem so talented or effective in the theatre. Steve McQueen's a good example. On the screen he has the remarkable ability to project himself."

Molly Picon was cast as Yente the matchmaker, and Norman's advice to her was "not to play her wildly comic. She should be a strong, intense, little old bent lady who represents the old traditions. She's very cunning, but she can be warm. Tevye's daughters see her in a different light, of course, almost as though she were a witch—which is how Tzeitel begins her imitation of Yente in 'Matchmaker, Matchmaker.' " Now in her seventies, Miss Picon is as spry as ever. She has repeatedly announced that she was retiring to concentrate on her gardening —only to change her mind because, as she explains, "tomatoes don't applaud."

Long before casting began, Joe Stein was at work on the screenplay; his participation had been part of the acquisition arrangement. "I worked with Joe for seven months," says Norman. "The first draft was almost exactly like the play. I didn't want to alter it too much; the play had been too successful to warrant changing any major plot points. But because film can and should provide a broader sweep than the stage, I wanted to open up all the large-scale scenes. For example, 'To Life' could begin in Lazar Wolf's home and continue as he and Tevye make their drunken way through the streets to Mordcha's inn, where the main portion of the dance would take place. The marketplace scenes could be filled with people, and the wedding of Motel and Tzeitel could be preceded by a big procession to the wedding site. And the exodus at the finale could suggest thousands of Jews leaving their villages all over the Ukraine."

A major change from the stage production was the way in which the rabbi was to be approached. The part had been created on Broadway by Gluck Sandor, a fey, funny and endearing little man who had been Jerry Robbins's first dancing teacher—which accounts for the rabbi's having an amusing dance bit during the wedding celebration. Because he was comic in a delightfully absentminded way, Sandor provided Jerry and Joe Stein with many opportunities to inject some gentle humor at the rabbi's expense. History was on their side, for in towns as poor as Anatevka, the peasants were rarely blessed with rabbis of great learning or stature; the best were off in more populous towns and major cities. Inevitably, Jerry and Joe received outraged letters from humorless conservatives who were shocked by the suggestion that a rabbi might be less than a Solomon. But in Robbins's stylization of the production, this approach to the character generally worked—even in Israel, though we did make an effort to give him more dignity.

Norman felt that the camera required a different approach. Since the synagogue would be real, as would the seriousness of religious studies and the solemnity of worship, the screen rabbi could in no way be a comic figure. In casting the role, Norman chose seventy-year-old Zvee Scooler, a man with a magnificently sensitive and craggy face and haunted eyes through which one could see the pain and wisdom of age. Scooler had been in Maurice Schwartz's 1921 Yiddish production of *The Dybbuk*, and five years later he and Paul Muni had made their English-speaking debuts together in *We Americans*. He was one of only two principal actors from the original cast of *Fiddler* to appear in the film. Leonard Frey was the other. But neither played the role he had created on the stage. Scooler had been Reb Mordcha on Broadway; Frey had played the rabbi's son, Mendel, the *shtetl's* chief reactionary, but in the film he moved up to the role of Motel.

Leonard Frey had originally auditioned for Jerry Robbins to play the role of Perchik, as Austin Pendleton had already been cast as Motel. Although Leonard hardly cut a figure as dashing and romantic as Bert Convy's, Jerry was sufficiently impressed with his ability to cast him as Mendel, a part Leonard has described as "originally no more than a cough and a mazel tov." In rehearsals, it became apparent that he was a first-rate

The rabbi (Zvee Scooler) and elders reading the Talmud in "Tradition."

talent, and as new lines and new scenes were being added, Mendel was invariably included in the action.

It's always hectic when changes are being made in a new show, and all the more so when actors have trouble absorbing them. Jerry and Joe could always count on Leonard's coming through quickly and effectively, without any fuss. When the "gossip sequence" and the final version of "Anatevka" were ready for rehearsal, it was almost a foregone certainty that Leonard would be given solos. This was a perfect example of how an alert, ambitious and talented actor can make his presence felt in a production that is taking shape. By the time *Fiddler* opened in New York, Mendel the rabbi's son had more onstage time than any other character in the show except Tevye.

Leonard understudied Motel as well as Perchik on Broadway, playing both parts many times. When Austin left the show after a year, Leonard took over officially as Motel and about the same time joined a new experimental theatre group led by Jerry Robbins. Jerry had received a generous foundation grant to work with a small company of actors to explore possible new ideas and new areas toward which to take acting, dancing and mime. Jerry searched in many directions, at times using masks and other stylized symbols, but apparently never found that elusive something he was looking for. The group was disbanded, but, says Leonard, "not before I'd gained valuable experience in parts ranging from Agamemnon to Jacqueline Kennedy—one of the most definitive characterizations of the century."

After leaving *Fiddler*, Leonard originated the role of the pockmarked homosexual, Harold, whose birthday was being celebrated by *The Boys in the Band*. It was an acidulous and compelling performance which he repeated in the film, and which established his reputation.

Norman originally hoped to find a very young actor to play Motel, and he tested several in Hollywood, including Artur Rubinstein's actor-son, John. He wanted the character to be tall ("not the expected tiny nebbish") with an innate dignity and promise, so that his transition to manhood would be entirely believable. Norman searched widely and finally decided that only Leonard Frey had the right physical look and also an inner feeling for the role. "I've looked all over the world," he told the actor, "but you're the only one who really connects with Motel."

When Tom Abbott returned to New York after shooting was over, he described a beautiful moment of Leonard's that had been captured on film. "Motel and Tzeitel run out of the barnyard after Tevye says they can marry, and you next see them running through a forest of white birch. The camera is tracking them as they run, and Leonard is in seventh heaven, swinging around the trees and swooping down to pick flowers. After they'd finished the scene, he said, 'You know, my childhood fantasy was that when I'd be in the movies, I would be running through the woods and a camera would be following me. And it's come true, it's come true. I'm in the movies!'"

When we were auditioning New York actors at Nola Studios on 57th Street, a young woman walked into our rooms one evening about six, just as we were leaving. She said she hoped to audition, and I was less than pleasant to her. I told her we were seeing actors through their agents and by appointment only. She started to leave, but I suddenly realized that her tallish figure, dark hair and oddly appealing face gave her a very Tzeitel-like quality. I stopped her and asked her to come back the next day. The following morning she returned, read and sang, and it was then we learned that she was currently understudying Tzeitel on Broadway. Norman was very impressed with her, and when he finally decided upon Leonard as Motel, it was obvious that Rosalind Harris would be the ideal Tzeitel to play opposite him.

In addition to Tommy, Leonard and Zvee Scooler, the only other veterans of the original stage production to be involved in the film were Larry Bianco, who repeated his role as the Russian dancer in "To Life," and Sammy Bayes, who assisted Tommy with the choreography and also danced in the major sequences. Neva Small, the film's Chava, might well have been in the original production had she shown up on a different day. On the audition lists for January 31, 1964, is the entry, "Neva Small, 11 years old." She had come in to be considered for either Bielke or Shprintze on a day when no one was at all interested in thinking about the children.

Among the hundreds of actors Norman saw before casting the role of Perchik was the young Israeli actor Assaf Dayan. Through a bizarre twist of fate, Dayan's scheduled audition involved us in a tragedy that blackened our lives for many days. It happened in February 1970, when Arab terrorists were beginning their violent harassment of international flights.

After Norman had auditioned all the New York actors I felt he should see, he, Lynn Stalmaster, musical director John Williams, Tommy and I flew to London to see English actors

Tevye's three marriageable older daughters. Above, from left to right: *Tzeitel (Rosalind Harris), Hodel (Michele Marsh), Chava (Neva Small).*

Norman Jewison, left, directing actors Leonard Frey (Motel) and Rosalind Harris (Tzeitel): the table-setting scene before the Sabbath meal.

and others from the Continent. Assaf Dayan had recently starred in films for John Huston and Jules Dassin, and Norman was considering him seriously enough to invite him to fly from Israel at the company's expense. One of Israel's leading actresses, Hannah Maron, had been suggested as a possible Golde (Norma Crane had not yet been cast), and though she was about to open in Tel Aviv as Lady Macbeth, she asked for and received two days off to test for the film.

The Mirisch Company's London office made flight arrangements for Dayan and Miss Maron, and we expected to see them at our audition hall (a synagogue in Soho) late in the afternoon of February 10. Their plane had one scheduled stop, Munich, and passengers were asked to leave the plane during the stopover. They waited in the passenger lounge without incident, but as they were boarding an airport bus to be driven back to their plane, a terrorist suddenly appeared and tossed a bomb into the bus, his target apparently being Dayan, son of Israel's Defense Minister, Moshe Dayan. One passenger was killed instantly. Dayan escaped unhurt, but Hannah Maron was injured critically. Except for a brief visit to London to meet Norman (under heavy security), Dayan remained by her side at the hospital. Two days later, word reached us in London that Miss Maron would live but that it had been necessary to amputate one of her legs.

Eventually, Michael Glaser was cast at Perchik after having been seen in the Broadway production of *Butterflies Are Free*. In a departure from tradition established by the stage production, Norman had Glaser play the part without a beard—the only Jew in the film to appear clean shaven—to accentuate Perchik's break from the old Orthodox traditions.

Long before shooting began, Norman was aware of a multiplicity of problems associated with producing a film musical. "Musical plays are indigenous to the theatre," he said, "not to film. In the theatre it is easier to accept a stylized, unreal atmosphere; film introduces the real world, with real scenery and real sounds. Audiences are more sophisticated now than they once were, and so most films are more realistic than ever. In film today, it is very difficult to use music and poetry and to suspend audiences' disbelief, as *The Wizard of Oz* once did so perfectly. That film made a brilliant and lasting impression on me in my youth."

After preliminary discussions with Norman, Tommy came away with a clear point of view as to the way *Fiddler* had to be handled on film. "As Norman told me, 'We can't have the villagers all lined up, coming down the road, singing "Tradition." ' In actually staging the dances, I did adaptations of what Jerry had done originally. I was given more dancers to work with than we'd ever had on the stage and much more space. It was really like starting fresh. I used the basic elements of Jerry's choreography for the dances themselves, but getting in and out of the numbers was something new—this was the big challenge. The idea was to make going into a dance as plausible as possible instead of, thump, suddenly starting to dance. I had to make each dance come out of the action logically and contribute something; then at the end I had to enable Norman to pick up the action again without any break."

Looking back on the past ten years of moviemaking, Norman says: "There have been very few good musicals on film—only *West Side Story, The Sound of Music, Mary Poppins, My Fair Lady* and *Funny Girl*. But look at the disappointments: *Dr. Dolittle, Paint Your Wagon, Star!, Camelot, Finian's Rainbow, Darling Lili, Sweet Charity, Goodbye, Mr. Chips, On a Clear Day You Can See Forever, Hello, Dolly!*"

According to Walter Mirisch: "The recent failure of so many movie musicals *has* given me pause. My own production of *How To Succeed in Business Without Really Trying* got good reviews but never caught on—why, I don't know. But even if I *had* started work on *Fiddler* later, after the *Star!–Dolittle*-type disasters, I would have gone ahead. The financing would have been more difficult to obtain, however."

Despite Mirisch's confidence in *Fiddler,* the economic squeeze that climaxed in Hollywood during recession year 1970 was such that though *Fiddler* wasn't shelved (as were, for example, *Say It With Music, She Loves Me* and *No Strings*), its projected costs were microscopically reexamined. As a result the initial $10 million budget was trimmed by 20 percent, which meant that Norman, as both the producer and director, had to adopt some shrewd cost-cutting procedures.

For one thing, he was more certain now than he'd ever been that he didn't want to shoot the film in Hollywood, and his decision was prompted as much by *Fiddler's* creative needs as by his own need to work with a reduced budget. He wanted the film to have the stamp of realism, not slickness. He wanted the wheat fields, the earth colors, the feeling of a place untouched by time or the twentieth century—effects he knew could never be simulated successfully in a studio. As critic Andrew Sarris put it, in his book *The American Cinema*, "Norman Jewison has been guided from the very beginning of his career by a commendable desire to escape from the confines of a studio set to the great outdoors of reality." Norman also wanted hardy peasant faces evocative of Eastern Europe rather than Central Casting. As a result, except for most of the principals, the majority of the cast was not American.

Firsthand investigation told Norman and his associate producer Patrick Palmer that the environment they wanted could be found either in Rumania, Yugoslavia, Hungary or Czechoslovakia. The landscape of each of those countries was closer to that found in Russia than anything that existed in the United States. After the Russian invasion of Czechoslovakia, however, the Iron Curtain countries were out of bounds to moviemakers; even if arrangements could have been made, insurance could not have been obtained by any film company wanting to work there. Austria was considered, but it was too mountainous, lacking the rural flatness Norman envisioned for the countryside around Anatevka. So, through elimination, Yugoslavia became the site for all exterior shooting. Because it is the most liberal of all Eastern-bloc nations, there were no insurance problems. Three ideal sites were found there, each within thirty miles of the town of Zagreb, where the company would be housed.

The *Fiddler* company headquartered in London, where all the musical numbers were prerecorded and rehearsed before shooting was scheduled to begin in Yugoslavia on August 10.

There, it was hoped, the camera would capture at least three seasons and the transitions between them, but 1970 weather conditions proved to be irregular in Yugoslavia and remained a constant problem from the day the company arrived. Although government meteorological reports were telephoned to the production four times a day, the weather itself seldom conformed to the predictions.

Each morning the production supervisor, Larry DeWaay, would arise at 4:30, check with the weather service and then drive to the projected shooting site. He would take an on-the-spot reading, but more often than not that would be fruitless and he would return to Zagreb to confer with Pat Palmer. Together—perhaps by doing some dexterous coin-flipping—they would decide where to send the company, the generators and the caravan of cars, trucks and buses that day. Amazingly little shooting time was lost in Yugoslavia, all things considered, but it was often necessary to "shoot around" the weather.

In November Norman planned to film November-like weather —gray skies and periodic rainfall. What he got instead was the most magnificent Indian summer on record: twenty-three days of sun for the month, instead of the twenty-eight and a half days of somber weather that meteorological reports had led him to expect. Late that month he had planned to shoot "Far From the Home I Love" in snow, because the countryside was supposed to be blanketed with whiteness by then. Predictably, there wasn't so much as a snowflake when it was time to film the number. Rather than lose time, Pat Palmer ordered the company back to London; they would all return to Zagreb once interior filming of the musical numbers had been completed.

Three weeks after the unit left Yugoslavia, five feet of snow lay unphotographed on the ground. It remained there until the very week the company returned; then it melted. "When we got back to Yugoslavia in February," says Norman, "the crocuses were coming up. We had no choice but to buy up all the available 'marble dust' in Eastern Europe and spray it on the ground and on all the trees and shrubs in camera range. Fortunately, the weather was still cold and the landscape bleak. The overcast sky was darker than the 'snow-covered' ground,

Fyedka (Raymond Lovelock) giving his book to Chava (Neva Small).

"We'll have to wait for the Messiah someplace else." The rabbi (Zvee Scooler) with son Mendel (Barry Dennen); Golde and Yente looking on.

so the scenes we shot then were believable. It was even cold enough to see the actors' breath as they spoke."

The village of Lekenik, which is built entirely of wood and has a Chagall-like quality in its random design, was used as the residential area for the fictional Anatevka. All that had to be built there was Tevye's house, barn and cheese hut, and these were deliberately constructed with tools and material that dated from the turn of the century, so that on film there would be no way to tell the old from the new, the real from the artificial.

The village of Martinska Ves, its architecture being totally Slavic (thus completely different from others in the area), became the Russian part of Anatevka. And the marketplace and synagogue were constructed in Mala Gorica. The clutter of shops and stalls that was fashioned there was so convincingly realistic that one day, at the peak of shooting, a local peasant tried to buy a horse.

Actually, as is the case with most locationing film units, a great many local residents became involved in the enterprise. Some worked as carpenters and laborers, others rented property to the company, and still others worked as extras in crowd scenes. "We rented their horses, their carts, chickens and ducks," says Tommy. "And not only were there crowds of natives in the wedding scenes, the marketplace and the exodus, but there was also a kind of stock company of villagers used all the way through. They were all very cooperative, but I'm sure a lot of what was happening seemed puzzling to them. There we were, in bright sunshine, with huge spotlights beaming down, and they couldn't understand why."

Despite the vagaries of the weather, most of the film was shot in Yugoslavia, including the musical numbers "Matchmaker, Matchmaker," "If I Were a Rich Man," "Tradition," "Miracle of Miracles," "Sunrise, Sunset," "Anatevka," "Far From the Home I Love" and parts of "Sabbath Prayer" and "To Life."

The other numbers were filmed at Pinewood Studios in England: the wedding and bottle dances, the dream sequence, "Do You Love Me?" and the main parts of "Sabbath Prayer" and

"To Life." The only two numbers from the original production that were not transferred to the screen were the gossip song, "I Just Heard," and Perchik's "Now I Have Everything" (which had been deleted from our stage productions in Israel and France).

After conversations with Jewison, Jerry Bock and Sheldon did write a new song for Perchik. "Musically I loved it," says Sheldon. "Jerry did a piece of music that had the quality of that marvelous old Russian folk song 'Meadowland.' We played it

"*Bottle Dance.*" Up center: *Perchik (Michael Glaser), Motel (Leonard Frey), Tevye (Topol), Tzeitel (Rosalind Harris), Golde (Norma Crane) and the guests at the wedding.*

United Artists

for Norman, and he liked it. I thought that at long last I'd solved the Perchik-song problem. Then Norman wrote us a month later and said he'd begun to feel the song had a quality of waving the Red flag, and could I change it. I did, and sent it off to him. Then they were recording it in England, and I got a phone call: Could I change it again? So I made changes and mailed them off. Then one day we got a letter saying they weren't using the song; it still had elements of Red flag-waving. I'd even bought a book called *Memoirs of a Revolutionary*, but

The ghost of the butcher's wife, Fruma-Sarah (Ruth Madoc), rising from the grave to terrify Golde in Tevye's bogus nightmare.

United Artists

I still couldn't solve the problem. I'm hopelessly middle-class."

Shooting was completed on February 12, 1971, but it would be nearly nine months before the editing, dubbing and musical scoring were completed. Several of the actors had to be dubbed entirely by other voices. The children who played Bielke and Shprintze sounded too British, and the Fyedka, Raymond Lovelock, had an Italian accent. (Although only twenty, Lovelock had already made several movies in Rome, and a recent poll in Japan had named him one of the three most popular movie stars there.)

While *Fiddler* was being edited, I asked Norman if he was

eager to do another musical. His immediate response: "God forbid!" Then he laughed and said, "No, I don't really mean that. If this one is successful, I'd like to do more. I enjoy working with music, but it would always depend on the book, on what *it* says." Norman had not sought to change the original conception of *Fiddler*, merely to open it up: to use his Panavision camera to enter the homes in the *shtetl*, to see and experience the daily lives of Jews in the village, to see the rich, broad expanse of European farmland—how hard the people worked there, how close they were to the earth and to their faith.

The medium of film had made it possible to enlarge and enliven the dream sequence—to have Tevye and Golde magically whisked off to a cemetery to confront the departed Grandmother Tzeitel and the butcher's wife, Fruma-Sarah. It was a chance to plunge into a stylized fantasy world and to incorporate the feeling of Chagall into the style, design and color of the sequence. The dream was the only portion of the film that Norman and his cinematographer, Oswald Morris, did not shoot through a silk stocking. For all the other scenes, they wanted warm brown earth tones, and the stocking successfully muted the colors of the landscape, the buildings and the costumes.

Inevitably, the screen *Fiddler* became more ethnic than the play. Research enabled Norman and his production staff to reconstruct in detail the actual world Sholom Aleichem lived in and wrote of. One question remained, of course: Would it all work?

What Jerry Robbins was able to *suggest* on the stage had to be *shown* on the screen. Jerry could be selective, but Norman had to fill the screen with realistic detail. The camera's very literalness was Norman's greatest obstacle in trying to retain those delicate and special qualities that had brought *Fiddler* so beautifully to life on the stage.

"I've had to be very careful with this one," Norman admitted to me. "Let's face it, if I don't bring it off, people will say, 'Look what Jewison ruined.' If I do bring it off, all they'll say is, 'Why not? It's a wonderful show.' The alternatives aren't great, but as Tevye might say, it's better to succeed than to fail."

People have said that *Fiddler* would not succeed in Amsterdam, in London, in Paris . . . and in nearly every place where it has moved and affected audiences so deeply. Hopefully, Norman Jewison's film will have been equally successful in reaching and touching people throughout the world.

But as Sholom Aleichem's Tevye once philosophized: "I never question God's way. Whatever He ordains is good. Besides, if you do complain, will it do you any good?"

Original Broadway Cast

FIDDLER ON THE ROOF *opened at the Imperial Theatre, New York City, on September 22, 1964, with the following cast:*

TEVYE, *the Dairyman*	Zero Mostel
GOLDE, *his wife*	Maria Karnilova
TZEITEL	Joanna Merlin
HODEL	Julia Migenes
CHAVA } *his daughters*	Tanya Everett
SHPRINTZE	Marilyn Rogers
BIELKE	Linda Ross
YENTE, *the Matchmaker*	Beatrice Arthur
MOTEL, *the Tailor*	Austin Pendleton
PERCHIK, *the Student*	Bert Convy
LAZAR WOLF, *the Butcher*	Michael Granger
MORDCHA, *the Innkeeper*	Zvee Scooler
RABBI	Gluck Sandor
MENDEL, *his son*	Leonard Frey
AVRAM, *the Bookseller*	Paul Lipson
NACHUM, *the Beggar*	Maurice Edwards
GRANDMA TZEITEL	Sue Babel
FRUMA-SARAH	Carol Sawyer
CONSTABLE	Joseph Sullivan
FYEDKA	Joe Ponazecki
SHANDEL, *Motel's mother*	Helen Verbit

and

THE FIDDLER	Gino Conforti

THE VILLAGERS

SHLOIME, *the Bagel Man*	John C. Attle
YITZUK, *the Streetsweeper*	Sammy Bayes
CHAIM, *the Fishmonger*	Lorenzo Bianco
DUVIDEL, *the Seltzer Man*	Duane Bodin
SURCHA	Sarah Felcher
LABEL, *the Woodsman*	Tony Gardell
HERSHEL, *the Potseller*	Louis Genevrino
YANKEL, *the Grocer*	Ross Gifford
SCHMERIL, *the Baker*	Dan Jasin
FREDEL	Sandra Kazan
YAKOV, *the Knifeseller*	Thom Koutsoukos
BERILLE	Sharon Lerit
MIRALA	Sylvia Mann
SIMA	Peff Modelski
RIVKA	Irene Paris
MOISHE, *the Cobbler*	Charles Rule
ANYA	Roberta Senn
YUSSEL, *the Hatmaker*	Mitch Thomas
SASHA	Robert Berdeen

Cast of the Film

The world premiere of the motion picture took place at the Rivoli Theatre, New York City, on November 3, 1971.

TEVYE	Topol
GOLDE	Norma Crane
MOTEL	Leonard Frey
YENTE	Molly Picon
LAZAR WOLF	Paul Mann
TZEITEL	Rosalind Harris
HODEL	Michele Marsh
CHAVA	Neva Small
SHPRINTZE	Elaine Edwards
BIELKE	Candy Bonstein
PERCHIK	Michael Glaser
FYEDKA	Raymond Lovelock
RABBI	Zvee Scooler
MORDCHA	Shimen Ruskin
CONSTABLE	Louis Zorich
AVRAM	Alfie Scopp
MENDEL	Barry Dennen
NACHUM	Howard Goorney
SHANDEL	Stella Courtney
GRANDMA TZEITEL	Patience Collier
FRUMA-SARAH	Ruth Madoc
PREVIOUS RABBI	Alfred Maron
THE FIDDLER	Tutte Lemkow
YUSSEL	Otto Diamant
SHEFTEL	Aharon Ipale
BERL	Brian Coburn
RIFKA	Marika Rivera
FARCEL	Stanley Fleet
GNESSI	Judith Harte
LEIBESH	Harry Ditson
MARCUS	Joel Rudnick
JOSHUA	Michael Lewis
HONE	George Little
REBECCA	Hazel Wright
ISAAC	Carl Jaffe
EZEKIAL	Mark Milicz
MOISHE	Arnold Diamond
BESS	Miki Iveria
ZELDA	Hilda Kriseman
BASHE	Sarah Cohen
NECHAMA	Susan Sloman
HEBREW SCHOOL TEACHER	Jacob Kalich
VIOLIN SOLOIST	Isaac Stern

Index